THE MINISTRY OF THE
WATCHMAN:

Beacon of the Body of Christ
Keeper of the Lord's Lighthouse

Barbara A. Williams

THE MINISTRY OF THE WATCHMAN:
Beacon of the Body of Christ,
Keeper of the Lord's Lighthouse

Published by Lighthouse Publishing Co.
Detroit, Michigan - Cleveland, Ohio

Page Layout and Cover Design, Shannon Crowley
Treasure Image & Publishing

Rev. Barbara A. Williams
The Ministry of the Watchman International
P.O. Box 43334
Cleveland, Ohio 44143
1-800-560-9240
www.ministryofthewatchman.com

Dedicated to the Chief Watchman,
Our Lord and Savior, Jesus Christ,
and to the Watchmen who serve with me
daily in Cleveland and Detroit.

To My Husband, Aubrey,
who watches out for me in every way.

THE MINISTRY OF THE WATCHMAN:

Beacon of the Body of Christ
Keeper of the Lord's Lighthouse

Introduction

For several years now I have wanted to put in writing the things that God has shown me over the past twelve years pertaining to this particular ministry. I hope that what you will read in this book will be enlightening, sobering, and informative. I hope it will encourage you to use the knowledge that is put forth here to help your work for the Lord Jesus Christ.

My work with this ministry began on an informal basis twelve years ago. At that time I was a member of a local church that you might call "partially spirit filled." That is to say, some people spoke in tongues, some "got quickenings," some jerked and danced when certain music was played, some just sat back and watched the whole thing bewildered. I was one of the latter group, with the exception that I spoke in tongues and was very active in a Charismatic women's fellowship as well. It was through this women's fellowship that I was exposed to the Word of Faith teachings, and the ministry of Rev. Kenneth E. Hagin, Sr. From reading brother Hagin's books I was able to learn about other dynamic people of the past whom God had used mightily to help the people of the earth come to a knowledge of God the Father through our Lord and Savior Jesus Christ. It was through the study of these works that I became familiar with the ministry of the Holy Spirit.

I began to see that it was because many people were mistaught or poorly taught on the word of God and the Holy Spirit and His gifts that much of the confusion in this church, as well as others, existed. People in this and many charismatic churches then and now came from varied religious backgrounds. Some people thought tongues was of the devil; others felt it was okay, but had little knowledge beyond that. Many pastors who had oversight of the flocks couldn't venture beyond what they were taught in seminary, so there was then and is now, much confusion in the church regarding the Holy Spirit, His ministry, and gifts.

It was the frustration at seeing this kind of ignorance and confusion among people who seemed to have a desire to serve God that motivated me to search the scriptures and the teachings of Spirit-filled Bible teachers past and present to gain understanding about the ministry, gifts and work of the Holy Spirit in the earth. I began to pray earnestly for understanding and truth, and God set me on a journey that led to my undertaking this ministry.

I can earnestly say that I never sought "my ministry." I knew that I was called to preach and teach The Word through a prophecy that I received at a Women's Aglow Fellowship meeting. Until that time, I had a "feeling" that I should do something for God, but no specific words had yet come to me. I sometimes chuckle at people who say that prophecy only confirms what the believer <u>already</u> knows. I honestly had no clue that I was called of God for certain nor did I know to what office I was called. Like many Christians, I had never considered being a preacher.

That was just not something one aspired to do. I had received my college degree in Nursing and Education, so I was amazed to know that I was actually called to preach and teach The Word of God.

Many people had come up to me in church and told me I was everything from a prophet to a preacher, but there was no Divine unction on their words that made the gift come alive inside of me until I stood before this woman at the meeting and asked if there was something God wanted to say to me. I laugh again at people who get rebuked for "asking for a word." Isn't it good that we serve a God who is smarter than all of us combined and knows how and what and when to speak to His beloved?

In subsequent months I received more confirmations and promptings from God to study more, pray more and share my goals as a Christian with my pastor, who invited me to pray weekly for the needs of the church with his wife. Thus began the ministry of the watchman as a personal ministry for that local church. We didn't call ourselves watchmen at that time. We were merely three women who met every week to pray for the church.

I began to notice a "pull" or "prompting" of the Holy Spirit to pray consistently at the same time each week. If I tried to put off that prayer time, I felt restless and upset inside. I

now know that the Holy Spirit was angry and restless--
"grieved" as we often call it. I also knew that we were
engaged in a type of prayer that had to be done regularly at
the appointed time and place. If the prayer was postponed,
it seemed that there was less time to get it accomplished,
and the services at the church were not as productive in
salvations, which was the main ministry done at the
church. There were no healing lines, no singing in the
spirit, no deliverance, and nobody asked for the baptism in
the Holy Spirit. Yet God did a work in me and through me
with our weekly prayer sessions. Our focus was always the
Sunday service, making it better, keeping the atmosphere
conducive to the work that we would pray for God to do.

I now know that our set prayer times were a "watch" given
by the Holy Spirit to us and that there was the maximum
grace (Divine enablement) to do the work if we kept the
given time. If we deviated from that appointed time, there
was less Divine enablement to do the watch, and it was less
productive.

I understand this in light of the Biblical references to the
watchman and His activities. A watch was always "set,"
just as a foot patrolman's "beat" is for a fixed time in a
fixed area. Not being consistent in time and place for a
watch is one of the primary reasons many people do not
undertake this ministry in a successful manner. God

demands first place, and He demands that His army be disciplined.

As we prayed weekly, I found developing within me a desire to see God do more. I began to get weary in praying for the same routine things over and over again.

I also began to discern certain spiritual activities and forces that seemed to dominate in the meetings. If I shared these with the pastor's wife, she seemed to be receptive to most of it, but at times would draw back from what I was saying. This new ability to see things accurately in the spirit and understand the forces behind the behaviors and activities that we observed marked my departure from strictly intercession to prophetic praying.

I knew that God was setting me on a different course. I was on a course of gathering information and understanding spiritual activity that I would later use in developing our prayers, prayer manuals, and teachings. These prayers affect spiritual activities in the heavenlies governing whole cities and regions, instead of just the atmosphere in one local church assembly.

I noticed that if I would pray against a certain spirit instead of praying about people, things, and needs, the effects would be more dramatic and on a larger scale than if I prayed for needs without addressing the spirit that was controlling and creating that need.

I made a decision to, as I told God one day, "quit chasing these impy gossip and lust devils every week and go after the strong man." I also committed myself to pray more of the word, and less things that I "thought" were needed. As I responded to the discipline of the Holy Spirit, a new ministry emerged within me. It was the ministry of the watchman.

The ministry of the watchman is a "set ministry" among the people of God and clearly defined in the scriptures. Its purpose is both governmental enforcement and protection both to the church and the world. The ministry of the watchman is a function of the school if the prophets, and is a part and foundation of the prophet's ministry.

I feel that all prophets should function in this ministry, as theirs is a ministry of intercession through revelation and the gifts of the spirit. It is because this ministry is clearly defined in scope, teaching, activities, lifestyle and discipline, that I have endeavored to keep records and write this book.

I believe that you will be as blessed as I am with understanding this unique and often misunderstood ministry. It is my desire to bring many others under the knowledge that God has given me of this ministry.

The Lord spoke some very important words to me that I seldom share with anyone, but I know they are true.

He said,

"I have called you as one who will study war. Many of my people will not study war ... they may engage in the fringes of minor skirmishes from time to time, but I need a people who will study war. If you will do this ministry for me, and teach it to others, and impart wisdom, and knowledge and anointings to my people, I will establish my future works in the earth with this ministry as a foundation. This ministry of the watchman will form the foundation for all ministry in the future."

Pretty strong words, huh? It's not my ministry, but His. I'm merely seeking to be faithful to teach it as He has given it to me. I hope this teaching will be useful to you as a foundation for your future life in Him.

Barbara A. Williams

CONTENTS

"Write the vision and make it plain upon tables that he may run that readeth it. For the vision is yet for an appointed time; But at the end it will speak, and it will not lie. Though it tarry, wait for it, for it will surely come, it will not tarry." Habakkuk 2:1-3

CHAPTER ONE

Prophetic Birthing of Ministry

THE VISION

How about that? A vision about a vision. But this is what God gave me as I prepared a proposal for a prayer ministry that I wanted to teach at the church. Until that time, I had prayed with the pastor's wife and another woman for about three years. I felt that I had been faithful to do what God called me to do in secret, but now He wanted me to teach it openly. Also, one of our prayer partners had quit and my sister, Shirley, had taken her place. We still prayed regularly, but I now felt a change was about to take place.

This has been a consistent occurrence in this ministry. When the leader is promoted, everyone under the leadership is promoted. Those who are not promotable (for whatever reason) will drop out. Also, when God plans a true promotion, the devil will sometimes come with a counterfeit promotion to move you off the right path.

The pastor had asked me to teach in the Sunday school program, but I felt that that was not what God wanted for me. I felt strongly that God wanted me to teach a very specific body of knowledge to His church. My only concern was whether or not the pastor would allow me to do this since I had declined his offer to teach Sunday School. Was I being arrogant, uppity, or even rebellious in wanting to teach what I felt I should teach? He would have to decide.

As I continued with the proposal, I wrote what I felt in my heart was God's plan to develop, not intercessors or prayer warriors, but a new breed of person of prayer who walked in an authority that kept evil spirits at bay. This new type of Christian would not be found putting on different pieces of armor and getting dressed for battle all the time, but would be armed and ready at all times to both defend and advance the Kingdom of Heaven. He would use man's God given power of dominion for the sake of the Kingdom of God and of His Christ. This person would be trustworthy, loyal, and kind to the sheep and shepherds, but would move in authority at the slightest move of the enemy. This person would be alert, awake, sober, and vigilant. This person would be a leader or layperson, male or female, educated or unlearned (in natural things) but highly knowledgeable and skilled in spiritual things and in the Word of God. He would endure hardships and be an overcomer. He would execute the written judgments of God against principalities and powers. He would be, in other words,

THE TERMINATOR

I'm sure that's what it sounded like to my pastor when I first began to speak about what I felt in my heart to do. I thank God that pastors are gifted to know what sheep really mean. Actually, the watchman is called to be all of the things I have described, but I don't think the average pastor or church is ready for this type of spiritual activity. One main reason is our lack of mental discipline in renewing our minds with The Word. Many times a spiritual vision can be met with a carnal or fearful interpretation. I don't know how many pastors would take to somebody raising a bunch of terminators in his congregation. However, he gave me the okay to start the meetings, and the ministry of the watchman was born.

Our first meeting was attended by about six or seven persons. I invited the pastor's wife, and of course, the lady who used to pray with us. The latter declined, saying (behind my back, of course) that she wasn't going "back to Egypt" and that God was moving her into the "teaching realm" herself. She eventually quit attending church altogether. The pastor's wife just seemed to be genuinely embarrassed at the thought that someone would see her listening to me teach. When we all prayed together, I guess we all thought we were leaders, even though the Holy Spirit would give me the areas to pray about and the revelation of the spirits behind the problem. Now that God had anointed me as a true leader, it was hard for these two ladies to take. I looked at my sister who had recently joined us, and I think I felt like Jesus when He asked the twelve, "are you going to leave me, too?" (John 6:67) I began to step into the prophet's reward … the dishonor he receives from his own countrymen (Mk. 6:4). The prophet will experience reactions of this type throughout his ministry. Extreme jealousy will be leveled at you because people value the anointing for the attention that it brings, but don't want to pay the price to attain it. Not everybody is called as a prophet, and will never have the anointing as you have it. Fortunately, my sister responded like Peter. She kind of felt she had no place else to go. It was in this ministry that she, like myself, felt life. So she has continued with me ever since.

THE ANOINTING BRINGS LIFE

Our meetings were alive with teaching on faith and The Word of God. The people were receiving the impartation of the anointing of God for prayer. They were encouraged and full of joy. I began to organize the prayers around the written vision. I would receive revelation as I read The Word regarding a spirit or pattern of demonic spiritual activity that was responsible for problems that we see in everyday life. For instance, in praying for drug addicts, The Holy Spirit revealed to me that the strongman behind this activity was the spirit of Pharaoh and that he uses witchcraft to pull people into the curse of early death.

I composed a prayer that incorporated this word of knowledge and wisdom into the prayer entitled "War on Drugs." Our prayers were written down and each one was prayed every time we met. We obeyed God's command to "write the vision and make it plain." We began to observe that anybody who saw the vision, (the prayer) written down would run with it, and run we did. We prayed twice a week corporately and in pairs. We would worship, prophesy, clap, pace around, bind the devil, strip him of his weapons, and divide his house.

Our prayer was more of a "drive by shooting" as we peppered the devil's house with a barrage of bullets from

The Word of God. We declared The Word so fast, that it left the devil dazed and in shock. Remember Hitler's BLITZKRIEG, or lightening warfare of World War II? The reason it worked is because it caught the victim totally by surprise. The devil is always surprised when Christians use their authority over him.

I taught faith principles that imparted strength into the hearts of the people. We didn't just talk about prayer. We did it. We prayed for our personal needs, got our own victories, and declared war in every area that God gave us. As time went on, one woman in the class volunteered to take our handwritten prayer cards home and copy them into her computer. At the end of her work, there were 59 prayers that formed our Master Prayer Manual.

I later added the teaching section to instruct people in how to use the manual. We used clippings from the local newspaper to chart the progress of our prayers. If a drug bust was reported in the paper, we clipped the story out of the paper and saved the clippings in a scrapbook. If drug activity increased, we saved that clipping, too, and beefed up the intensity of the prayer in that area.

When newcomers or visitors came to the meetings, we had them join in and pray the prayers. We first made sure they were baptized in the Holy Spirit and prayed in tongues.

This is a sign of a believer, (Mk 16:18). We also made sure people knew we were not a "prayer service," to take the responsibility of prayer off them, but a ministry that was called to teach them to pray and impart life, faith, strength and hope to the believer. We boldly told people, "we will help you by teaching you to pray for your own needs by using the prayer of agreement."

Because of God's unique blessing over agreement (Matthew 18:19), we began to see dramatic results. We used this simple method: One person prayed from the pre-written prayer card in the understanding and the other person agreed by praying in tongues. This caused a very distinct anointing of power to come upon us as we prayed. That has been a trademark of the ministry.

The more word we prayed, the stronger the anointing became. If anyone deviated too much from the written prayer, and drifted into his own thoughts, the anointing would begin to lift, and the person praying in tongues would get stronger in tongues and bring that person back into the spirit. We began to see tongues as our power source or balancer to keep us in the Spirit. This is why it became mandatory that persons receive the baptism in the Holy Ghost. People who were not Spirit-filled came to our meetings to receive tongues.

In this way we were able to pray the revelation of God in the understanding and pray the perfect will of God and edify our spirits by praying in tongues. This type of prayer has created in the watchmen a military-type discipline that has kept the prayer in the spirit and out of the soul. Thus the watchman as a true soldier in the army of God has developed. A true soldier is fully equipped to do the work of the ministry.

A type of discipline began to develop in our personal lives. More and more we were given over to seeking out things that kept us in the flow of the spirit of God. I asked the pastor for money to purchase our first set of books, a Kenneth Hagin Library. We studied faith, prayer, The Word, and the anointing and started our own book and tape library, since we taped what I taught. The watchmen were eager to learn more about the ministry and committed to study The Word in their spare time. We were happy about our work for the Lord. Happy, that is, until the devil retaliated. We entered our first ...

And the watchmen of Saul in Gibeah of Benjamin looked; and, behold, the multitude melted away, and they went on beating down one another. 1 Samuel 14:16

CHAPTER TWO

Prophetic War:
The Spirit of Religion vs. The Holy Spirit

"How dumb can you be, Barb?" I thought to myself. "Nobody gets to punch the devil out forever. Remember, 'we *wrestle* against principalities and powers,' (Eph. 6:12)."

If scripture doesn't help you, then remember Newton's third law of motion: **FOR EVERY ACTION THERE IS AN EQUAL AND OPPOSITE REACTION.** For the action that we were taking in the spirit, the devil was responding with his opposite reaction.

So there I was in the pastor's office answering a bunch of questions about what I was teaching the people. Even though I had offered to give him the tapes of each class, (which he refused) I was here defending myself against the accusation of the devil.

As I sat and listened to the charges against me, which ran along these lines, "Elder Loudmouth tells me that your people act like they know more than everybody else ..." "We're trying to keep unity here ..." "Who is Kenneth Hagin? I've never heard of him ..." "I just don't want you to get off ..." "Well, what I've noticed is all your people seem to be spiritually arrogant ..."

I felt impressed to tell the pastor that I didn't feel the people were arrogant. I felt that faith makes a person adamant in what they believe, and that they were merely saying what they believed The Word of God to be saying and they were convinced of it, where perhaps others weren't as convinced ...

Well, you would have thought I slapped him. All of a sudden this angry rage came upon his face. I'd seen that before. Once, when I was talking about casting out devils and asked him if he believed in the ministry of deliverance, that same angry "thing" began to well up. I'd heard that angry thing preach on many occasions.

It was a religious spirit. It had attacked me before. If I disagreed with the pastor regarding something in The Word, he'd pick up that religious thing and retaliate with accusations of witchcraft, causing division, usurping authority over a man, the whole gamut. I never knew why he didn't see it and seek deliverance.

He even admitted once that because he was raised Methodist, he had a lot of religious spirits "*around* me but not *in* me," as he put it. I have yet to understand the difference, especially when you obey them, and let them use you.

I finally said, "Pastor, what do you want me to do? Should I quit?"

"No, no, no. I'm just telling you what others have said. You do good things. You know I respect your gift …"

He always referred to "my gift," as though it was something that operated independent of me as a person. I found that people are impressed with gifts, yet everybody has one. The Bible says that your gift will make room for you. (Prov. 18:16). I don't think he really understood my "gift," as he put it, even though he was the pastor.

Over the years I have observed how ignorance concerning God's Kingdom, and the fragmentation in the ministry of the five-fold gifts has left the church powerless and in strife, confusion and frustration. In The New Testament church that Jesus birthed, the apostle is the chief overseer, not a denominational board. In the church at Antioch, there were prophets and teachers as well as pastors (Acts 13:1). Evangelists worked primarily on the outside preaching to gather in the sheep, but so did the apostle. The church of today bears little resemblance to the one Jesus started.

Today, through tradition, the dominant gift is that of the pastor, who is appointed by a board, not a ministry gift office like that of the apostle or prophet. We seldom see or recognize any other ministry gift.

The evangelist is recognized because their ministry helps to bring in new converts, but the ministry of the teacher had been relegated to Sunday School teaching and was not considered of equal importance with that of the pastor. The ministry of the prophet has been almost unheard of over the years because it is very direct, confrontational and actually primary and foundational to the body of Christ.

The Bible states a rank, or order of ministry gifts, the apostle being first and prophets second.

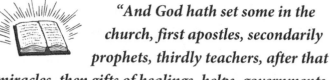

"And God hath set some in the church, first apostles, secondarily prophets, thirdly teachers, after that miracles, then gifts of healings, helps, governments, diversities of tongues." 1 Corinthians 12:28

So how did this upside-down order in the church occur?

REVERSE ORDER IN THE CHURCH

Through persecution the church suffered a fragmentation, or dispersing. God always restores what belongs to Him, and as God began to move to restore the church, men began to set up governing boards and denominations to regulate the work. This regulation was done without respect to office, gift, or calling.

Actually, many persons set up denominations based on one truth instead of the full gospel, and men were hired because they had graduated from the denominational seminary, and were indoctrinated to a specific set of beliefs, instead of a belief in God's Word.

Denominations have such a stronghold in religious life, that people have described themselves according to denomination instead of faith. It is because these man-made systems intertwine with the church that there is often conflict between leaders who do not have the ability to discern gifts by their characteristics and respect the call of God on a life that carries a specific gift.

But there are still apostles and prophets called into the ministry today, because Jesus is the same yesterday, today, and forever. It is *this* church, the one that embraces the ministry of the apostle, prophet, evangelist, pastor, and teacher that the gates of hell will not prevail against, because this church is perfected and matured, and equipped for the ministry.

"And he gave some, apostles; and some, prophets; and some, evangelists; and some, pastors and teachers; For the perfecting of the saints, for the work of the ministry, for the edifying of the body of Christ: Till we all come in the unity of the faith, and of the knowledge of the Son of God, unto a perfect man, unto the measure of the stature of the fullness of Christ: That we henceforth be no more children, tossed to and fro, and carried about with every wind of doctrine, by the sleight of men, and cunning craftiness, whereby they lie in wait to deceive;"
Ephesians 4:11-14

Jesus is Lord over this church, so it is founded on The Rock. He is not Lord over man-made systems. Man is. Whenever man decides to set up a government that is not based on The Word of God, the full effects of the power of the gospel are not present. This lack of power to heal, set free, and see miracles will remain as long as churches are served by one gift only. In order to bring people into maturity, teaching and preaching from all five ministry gifts is necessary.

WHO'S YOUR SOURCE?

When men lack ability, they will use whatever means necessary to make up for that lack. I see this in the church. Pastors who do not rely exclusively upon the Holy Spirit for information and guidance will be open to receive knowledge from almost anywhere. I've found it to be true over the years that people who form their opinions from gossip begin to lose their grip on reality.

They are easily beguiled, because they don't really trust God to inform and direct them as leaders. They tend to be emotionally led, and are easily upset and moved by what they hear. When I began to minister, God warned me to stay away from men's opinions and their gossip. I've learned that if you get your information from God, He'll give you instruction for the sheep that will help them. Man's information leads to failure.

In talking with the pastor, it was very difficult for me to know what (if any) changes I needed to make in my teaching, since he could not make any concrete suggestions. He merely wanted to let me know what was being whispered about me. This is a sign of emotionally led leadership. Gossip defiles one's spirit and will make you dependent upon the next morsel of gossip for your information.

Pretty soon, you have chaos and a house of confusion, because God is not the author of gossip and complaints. Leaders who are led by the Spirit of God know how to direct, teach, encourage, and correct the other ministers in their congregations. They know how to bring out the best in others and help get them equipped for their ministry. Godly leadership leads people to prosper. It does not stifle a person's growth and ability to function in their calling.

EFFECTS OF RELIGIOUS TRADITION

Religious tradition can be a killer of new ministry. Since my pastor had come from a denominational background and had grown up in the church, he based much of what he did on the traditions of the church in which he grew up. These traditions had kept him blinded regarding his own salvation. He was born again after he went to college, and had a real encounter with God. As it is with most denominational churches, salvation seems to be the only experience most converts have had with God.

Since the Azusa Street revival of 1904-1906, God has led His people into the fullness of His Spirit, which many of us refer to as the baptism in the Holy Ghost. This experience also involves the release of the gift of speaking in other tongues as the Spirit of God gives utterance. This little member, the tongue gets us into a lot of trouble whether we use it for God of not.

I recognized that many people in our church were not baptized in the Holy Ghost, but the pastor always told me that *he* was and that he was "for" the experience. Somehow he still seemed to be confused regarding the Holy Spirit, His gifts, and what believers should do for God. Once he publicly admitted to the entire church that he had fooled himself into thinking that he was baptized in the Spirit, but had never spoken in tongues.

Prior to that confession, he would get up and argue over and over again that you received all of the Holy Ghost when you're saved. "Baptism means 'identification'," he would say. Of course this left everybody more confused than before, but he fought conviction as long as he could. He finally begged God to baptize him in the Holy Spirit and spoke in tongues, but he never appeared to grow in ministry or receive teaching beyond that.

This is a very dangerous and grave mistake. God's power follows knowledge. Where there is knowledge and study of the Word, you will find the release of His power. Leaders who open themselves up to gifts without pursuing knowledge for the administration and uses of that gift are in danger of leading people astray and will wind up condemning the gift as worthless.

For instance, if I give you a gold nugget and you have no idea that it is gold or that gold is valuable, you my toss it outside thinking that it is just another rock. If you are not taught the value of it and how to treasure it, you will not receive the full benefits of its ownership. It is the same with the gift of the Holy Spirit.

If you do not understand all that each gift enables you to do, you will begin to treat this as a light thing. The gift of tongues actually unlocks the door to higher faith and strengthening of your spirit man. Higher gifts of the Spirit, (like the words of wisdom, words of knowledge, and miracles), become accessible and the anointing and knowledge to administer them come as well. Praying in the Spirit keeps you in the love of God and causes you to walk in the spirit of the faith of Jesus (Jude 20-21).

I share this with you because this lack of knowledge and conflict over knowledge among ministers is a common occurrence in many churches. Prophets need a place where they can grow and be taught accurately the things pertaining to their ministry. While pastoring is necessary for all, there will always come a time when those of us who are serious about God need and desire teaching that goes beyond the pastoral abilities.

That is why teaching ministers have such large meetings. The Kenneth Hagins, Copelands, Marilyn Hickeys, and Joyce Meyers of the earth are called by God (there are others, as well) to fill that void that only the teaching office can fill. Brother Hagin serves in the Office of the Prophet, as well, so his ministry was able to lay the foundation for the Word of Faith movement that we are receiving the benefit of now.

We all need teaching to move beyond the level of receiving care, which is the main focus of the pastor's gift. We need vision, impartation, and understanding. These abilities come from the offices of the Prophet and Teacher.

GOD RESOLVES THE CONFLICT

I prayed for our pastor regularly in those days. I could see him struggling with something that he couldn't get free of. He seemed to be bound in the "salvation only" mentality, even though he genuinely seemed to desire the full gospel ministry of Jesus. Once he had a healing meeting where he prayed for the sick and God healed them, but he never continued to study the healing ministry. I found that learning the ministry of Jesus is something that a person has to adopt as a life's work. This knowledge does not come "automatically."

I also realized that the pastor was fighting a religious spirit, and that most of the several hundred persons in the church carried the same religious spirit. Religious people seem to be hungry for power, but not for the right reasons. They always seem to be trying to "prove something."

Anointed people are a threat to religion. The anointing brings liberty. Religion binds. In the anointing there is strength and life. In religion there is death. Spirit-filled people walk in the spirit. Religious people walk in the flesh; sometimes it's nice and well behaved flesh, but flesh just the same.

In spite of our differences in understanding regarding the Holy Spirit, I thought God would find a way for me to do my ministry in the church since the pastor was the one who initiated my serving as a minister. I prayed for an answer from God regarding this latest conflict.

The Lord showed me the conspiracy of the devil to abort and kill the ministry that He had given me. Jealousy is an evil. It severs people from one another and causes spiritual pain to persons toward whom it is aimed. The Bible says that for envy the Pharisees delivered Jesus to Pilate. (Matthew 27:18). Religion and envy cause spiritual blindness. The spiritually blind do nothing but relate to natural, carnal things.

Unfortunately, pastors sometimes become dependent upon other people's observations about the flock and not God's. Their ears can become more sensitive to gossip than to the voice of the Holy Ghost. My pastor fell victim to this evil, and I felt more and more like an outsider.

One weakness that I had a hard time overcoming was a feeling of rejection. Because of their sensitivity to spiritual things, prophets often feel this way (1 Samuel 8:7). I had never really felt accepted by the elders, deacons, or the pastor there. I always felt tolerated, and grossly misunderstood.

I once heard Brother Mike Murdock say, "Go where you're celebrated, not where you're tolerated." Good advice. Only I didn't know that back then. I felt this conflict of wanting to go and wanting to stay. I knew then and now that I was engaged in a battle of the spirit of religion vs. the Spirit of God.

THE SPIRIT OF RELIGION

If Religion is all you're ever exposed to, then that's all you know. Religious folks have very little exposure to the real power of God, and actually come under conviction for their falseness when the truth shows up. They fight the real because they don't know how to apprehend it, contain it, or work with it.

The real can only be submitted to. The religious will offer positions to people who are anointed in an attempt to control the anointing that they carry. They may even appear to have no respect for the anointing when it rests upon another person. They only like control.

Unfortunately, they're not aware that what they have is false. If they are born again, God can use them at times where they are yielded to Him. There are other times when they merely "go through the motions," of ministry, and they lack results.

They think they've got God, and are quick to accuse the anointed of being involved in witchcraft, because *they* do not have the supernatural power of God working in *them*. There are little or no signs to confirm the ministry that they do. No casting out of devils, no healings, no, or very little speaking in new tongues.

 *"And these signs shall follow them that believe; In my name shall they cast out devils; they shall speak with new tongues; They shall take up serpents; and if they drink any deadly thing, it shall not hurt them; they shall lay hands on the sick, and they shall recover." Mark 16:17-18*

After I was born again, God taught me His Word and healed me of a severe depression, so I've always sought a demonstration and power ministry just like the one Jesus had and said we are to do. I was never willing to compromise what I knew to be the revealed truth of God's Word. I thought everybody loved and respected Brother Hagin and the work that he has done to bring the knowledge of faith to all of us.

I was shocked when the pastor stood in the pulpit and said, "Kenneth Hagin is not the pastor of this church. If you like him so much, see if he'll bury you." Things seemed to be getting out of hand. Here was a man who said he loved God on one hand and could preach salvation, but seemed to hate anybody and anything that spoke of the healing and deliverance ministry of the Lord Jesus Christ. I was ready to move on at any time.

Instead of letting me leave, God gave me a new strategy for prayer. He gave me a new prayer aimed at protecting the ministry from the evil of jealousy, false accusation and hatred from believers. I called it the "Seven Abominations" taken from Proverbs 6:17.

We began to pray the prayer. The tension and accusation of the devil began to die down among the brethren, but the pastor seemed to be more angry and withdrawn. I would think of Nebuchadnezzar and how the Bible says he looked when Schadrach, Meschach, and Abed-Nego refused to bow to the image they were told to worship. The Bible says, "He was full of fury and the form of his visage changed." (Dan. 3:19).

I understand how the devil infects and stirs up evil among the brethren. It's a bad thing for a leader to let the devil's gossip control his mind. Fellowship with spiritual people if you want to be spiritual. If you associate with carnal, you will be carnal. Once the devil has a grip on your soul, he can command and stir you up to do anything.

After one year in existence at that church, we found the church door locked one day when we showed up for prayer. That didn't surprise me. The pastor had long since quit speaking to me about the ministry. When I came into church, I would see deacons and elders in the corners whispering. They stopped when they saw me. I continued to stay because God had not told me to leave, but when the church door was locked, I felt free to leave. I never went back, and never looked back.

GOOD-BYE PHARAOH

Backbiting is a terrible sin. It's a sign of impotence and fear. After our one talk in his office, the pastor never spoke to me face to face about the ministry again. I heard later that he told the congregation that he had to "sit me down"; that I had "gotten beyond my gift…" whatever that means.

You know, the Word of God warns us not to even judge another man's servant (Romans 14:4). God is able to make a servant of His stand or fall. Pastors have the authority to ask other ministers to minister *in their church, only*, or ask them not to, for they are the door of the sheep, but they cannot "sit down" someone from ministry, because they did not raise them up.

Only Jesus, as the head of the church can do that. We must all be careful with what we say to encourage or discourage people in the ministry. If you read the Bible, the ministry of discerning gifts and callings belongs more to the prophet than to any of the other ministry gift offices, and even prophets cannot forbid someone to start a church or a ministry. If they receive a word from God along these lines, it will come with instruction that helps a person prepare himself for ministry before he steps out if he is called, or it will help that person accept his true calling.

Once a person is anointed by God to stand in a ministry gift office, our position must be "hands off." It is dangerous to speak against the anointed of God, to tell people not to attend their meetings or try to discourage people from receiving them, since the anointing represents the approval of God. (1 Samuel 16:1-13).

The pastor warned his congregation not to come to my meetings. It reminds me of what Pharaoh told Moses and the children of Israel when God finally led them out of Egypt. He always sends you off with a threat or a curse. "If you leave this place, evil is before you (Ex. 10:10)."

He called other pastors in the city and "warned" them about me, so I was persecuted in the next church I attended. Every wicked device the devil could contrive, he threw at me, but we continued to meet and pray. We first met in the home of a very wonderful pastor's wife, then in the recreation room of the apartment where one of the watchmen lived, then in one church, then another. With each move, we gained strength and numbers.

That was ten years ago. We are now an international ministry comprised of two chapters with two weekly, and one monthly meeting. We also teach healing schools six times per year in three cities. We've ordained our first minister, (my sister), and we have twice-yearly conferences that feed the sheep the real, pure unadulterated word of God in demonstration and power of the Holy Ghost.

We are a school of the prophets, so there we provide a place where young prophets and watchmen can be trained instead having their call aborted in Pharaoh's house. I preach in churches, conferences, at Women's and Men's Fellowship meetings, and any place God sends me. I am able to do this all because we refused to back down to Pharaoh and his "Jezebel" elders. These wars are meant to destroy you, your reputation, and your spirit. But we serve a God to stands up for His anointed, and will fight with you and for you, just as He did for us. To Him is the glory.

If you are called as a prophet or watchman, or to any five-fold office, or you want to learn how to function in your ministry for God, He has provided a place for you to be trained, so continue to seek it. But remember, all hell will come against you, sometimes even through your trusted leaders.

Don't be shocked if your greatest enemies are among your brethren. We all keep saying we're in the end times. Well, Jesus warned us that one of the signs would be that "many will betray one another" (Matthew 24:10) because of offenses. I realize that my teaching The Word and moving in the power of God in a church where the pastor and none of the elders had this ability offended them.

I also know that if I had to do it over again, I would not change a thing. It was also said of Jesus that He would be a stone of stumbling and a rock of offence (Romans 9:33). When He begins to move on one of His servants, it will offend those who don't know Him in certain areas of ministry.

My prayer is that none of us ever again stumble at the stumbling stone. I pray that we recognize and discern His body; that we respect the anointing and call of God upon one another and move spiritually and not carnally.

He calleth to me out of Seir, Watchman, what of the night?
Watchman, what of the night? Isaiah 21:11

CHAPTER THREE

Who Is The Watchman?

People come up to me at meetings where I preach and tell me that God has told them they are watchmen. Seldom do I find anyone who can tell me anything about this ministry. They always say, "I'm a watchman on the wall." Sometimes I think, "*off* the wall is more like it." It's amazing how believers feel that somehow ministry comes naturally.

We'll think nothing of going to medical school, law school, or even driving school to learn our trade, but seldom do we think of a school of ministry if we are called to ministry. Or, we assume that we'll be taught everything we need to know in the local church setting. Traditionally, the local church is designed for the care and nurturing of the sheep, and not for teaching ministers. It did not begin this way, but down through the ages, the church has changed.

Unfortunately most local churches are one-gift oriented. The pastor preaches, teaches, counsels, and administers. It takes the ministry of all five to mature us and prepare us for ministry (Eph. 4:11-12).

Some people will come out of their comfort zones of Sunday/Wednesday services for a little refreshing at a conference, but are reluctant to commit to consistent teaching. Our traditions hinder us sometimes from seeking to be properly trained for our ministries.

FUNCTIONS OF THE WATCHMAN

So who is the watchman? The Watchman is one who is assigned a specific list of duties in prayer and warfare that have the following functions for the body of Christ: **protection, defense, observation, warning, revelation, offense, execution of written judgments upon principalities and powers, establishing Divine government of the church, preparing the way of the Lord, and carrying out the Word of the Lord.**

As you can see, these duties are consistent with the office of the prophet, and where some duties had a natural execution under the old covenant, they have *spiritual executions* under the New Covenant.

As a function of the school of the prophets, then, the ministry of the watchman would include all the ministries of those who comprised the company of prophets. Those are prophets who stand in the office, sons of prophets, minstrels, psalmists who worked with prophets, servants, priest, and prophets in training. The school, or formal training ground for the prophets and their assistants and students, was not in operation until Israel was called out as a nation and given the law.

There is some evidence that the prophet's office was responsible for the training of all ministers including the priests. The prophet Samuel, because Eli, the priest, trained him probably was the first to blend these two ministries, or cause the ministers to come under the teaching of a senior prophet. It appears that his home at Ramah was a place where companies of prophets were housed and trained. Throughout the history of Israel, the prophet is recognized as the head of the groups of ministers. His office was subordinate only to God. This is what earned the prophet the description as "God's servant, the prophet" (Jer. 7:25).

Moses, the prophet, was the first man given instructions for the tabernacle and the priests' office, and he taught these duties to Aaron and his sons. Prophets often set up altars and made sacrifices to the Lord. So the prophet was also a priest, but not necessarily of the line of Aaron. Prophets had no particular genealogy. God chose them sovereignly, often before they were formed in the womb (Jeremiah 1:5).

God seeks out watchmen.

"And I sought for a man among them, that should make up the hedge, and stand in the gap before me for the land, that I should not destroy it: but I found none."
Ezekiel 22:30

The first requirement is that God must seek out and find one who is willing to respond to the call of the watchman. All watchmen must be called of God. Not all intercessors are watchmen, as you can see from the functions listed above. So the first qualification of the watchman is that God must call him. When God calls one as a watchman, he is called to do a specific function of intercession, but that person must go a step farther and carry out duties that are characteristic of this intercessory prayer ministry.

The watchman prays, as do all believers. Prayer is merely the act of communicating with God in such a way that God responds with some action of intervention in the affairs of earth. Prayer brings about the will of God.

A watchman intercedes, as one who *stands in the gap* on behalf of the land. The watchman, however, in standing in the gap, finds that there are a myriad of activities associated with that. As he stands in the gap, he finds that God then begins to have him carry out other duties.

This may require him to speak to key people in the earth The Word of the Lord. The watchman then becomes God's messenger to the people.

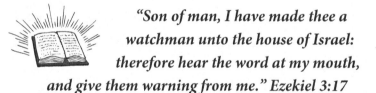 *"Son of man, I have made thee a watchman unto the house of Israel: therefore hear the word at my mouth, and give them warning from me." Ezekiel 3:17*

This is a function of the prophet's ministry.

THE SENIOR WATCHMAN

The prophet, then, as the senior watchman, or leader of the school or company of prophets, receives the *job description* that pertains to this ministry of the watchman. From the outline of the duties that he has received from the Lord, the prophet is able to obtain the burden of the Lord for the land.

This burden may consist of confronting a specific area of demonic activity like witchcraft. While confronting this evil, he may find that drug abuse, child abuse, family discord and perversion all come under the heading of witchcraft. It is the prophet's job, then, to get a strategy from the Lord to defeat and dethrone this evil as a dominant power in his territory.

The warfare that the prophet is engaged in is then a *governmental warfare aimed at defeating a Prince who rules a principality or a strongman that controls an area of thought, ideology or area of interest. The prophet must be willing to confront on all levels of demonic power. His main target, however, is the Prince or strongman in a city, region, or country.*

This level of warfare that the prophet engages in is a result of his position of being a "sent one" in the Kingdom of God. All prophets are foundation-laying ministers.

"And are built upon the foundation of the apostles and prophets, Jesus Christ himself being the chief corner stone."
Ephesians 2:20

As such, the prophet must lead the way for the rest of the body of Christ in entering into new revelations, higher demonstrations of power, or renewal and reemphasis of certain truths from the Word of God.

The prophet "prepares the way of the Lord," through prayer, fasting, announcing (preaching) and watching for the coming of the Lord. The Lord comes in many ways. He comes in the flesh, in pre-incarnate form, in theophany, in types, shadows, in a whirlwind, in a revival, in an outpouring, or in a new revelation given through His spokesmen.

The Lord must always be announced before he comes, and must have someone who knows and watches for his appearing to announce him. This new appearance of the Lord lays a new foundation for the building of the church. It may be a new foundation of a truth that has been perverted, or hidden, or stolen from the people of the earth, or it may be an expansion and clarification of present truth. The prophet preaches and declares until the Body has received the Word.

The prophet as watchman must have eyes to see what the Lord wishes to show him and ears to hear what the Spirit is saying to the church. He digs a foundation of truth with his tongue through preaching what he sees and hears in the spirit. He must proclaim this truth to whomever God sends him. This includes demonic princes and lesser spirits. Because of his access to Divine revelation through his gift, the prophet carries light for the rest of the body of Christ.

Prophets seem to be what I call "alive from the neck up," having the ability to sense spiritually through the eyes, ears, and of course, to proclaim through the mouth, the wisdom of God. It is the revelation, or light that they carry and walk in that gives vision and direction to the rest of the body of Christ, and is what causes the reaction of fear that many people experience in their presence. (Deuteronomy 18:22).

In the Bible we see the Prophet Moses confronting the wicked Pharaoh in order to obtain the release of God's people from the land of Egypt. The man Pharaoh was really under the influence of the Prince of Egypt, the Spirit of Pharaoh. Demonic princes rule seats of authority. We confront the spirit of Pharaoh now in our prayers.

We find this spirit in operation doing the same things to the people of God that he did to them in Moses' day. Pharaoh is responsible for the abortion of gifts and callings in the church, just as Pharaoh aborted the Hebrew male babies.

This spirit causes natural abortions as it works in our government and legislature. It is tied in with the spirit of humanism, and so gives people false ideologies to believe and adhere to, to make its murderous ideas sound logical, humane, intelligent, and necessary.

Pharaoh puts heavy burdens upon the people (Ex. 1:11), making them too weak and oppressed to worship and serve the Lord. The current hurried lifestyle that most people live, with little time to spend with the family and even less time to spend with God is one created by the Spirit of Pharaoh's influence. This spirit influences seats of authority and leadership whether they are in the home, government, the church, or the workplace.

GOD'S STRATEGY AGAINST PHARAOH

Let's study how God deals with this spirit. When Moses was a baby, God moved on the heart of Pharaoh's daughter who saw Moses lying in an ark caught in the bulrushes, to rescue him and bring him home with her. This is a picture of the church in the world. We are "caught," so to speak, in a world that is alien to us, but we have a Divine purpose here as salt and light. God will often place the deliverer smack-dab in the middle of the lap of the Principality. We need to be here to study the enemy's tactics. Christians need to wake up.

We will never get victory by being nice to everything. God sends prophets into the very seat of the activity he wants to overthrow. If a church is teaching a watered-down or inaccurate gospel, God will send a baby prophet there to learn what is being taught. Then he will take that person aside and teach him his ways. Or God may decide to send someone who is grounded in his truth there to sit, watch and pray.

If the pastor or other minister in charge properly recognizes that prophet, a very productive relationship will result. The prophet will work along with the other ministers, and bring his vision and direction where necessary. The problem is, many ministers don't like correction, even from a minister who is on their level. We don't hold ministers in high enough esteem to be able to humble ourselves and allow their ministry to come upon the people. God wants a perfected church.

You need to know that he has placed wise persons in the earth and given them gifts of discernment so that they will be able to pray prayers that will allow a greater degree of truth to come to His people. Prophets come to aid the church by bringing truth and revelation to her. We are not here to tear down what God has built, but to build it stronger.

Prophets are often raised in Pharaoh's house. Many of us have been given "the left foot of fellowship" from a church, even as young or fledgling prophets, by the spirit of Pharaoh. Often if Pharaoh can't abort your call before you're anointed, he will kick you out with a warning, and cause you to run fearing the pursuit of his chariots and horsemen (Ex. 14:8)

The Prophet Elijah had perhaps the most confrontational and dangerous of ministries by having to confront the pagan, idolatrous couple Queen Jezebel and King Ahab (1 Kings 18). Because these people were leaders over God's heritage, Elijah's job was very dangerous. Elijah had to know his place as a servant of God, yet obey God in order to deliver the people.

He had to know that it is the prophet's job to expose and confront evil, no matter who is doing it. Much of the teaching afoot in the church today regarding the prophet's ministry is an attempt to diminish this powerful governing ministry in scope, ability and authority.

Wisdom should admonish us to "do God's prophets no harm" (1 Chronicles 16:22). The prophet is very jealous for God. This jealousy causes a zeal in the prophet to carry out the Word of the Lord.

So the watchman, then, is one who has a specific call on his life to carry out governmental warfare, and has intercession and prayer that is prophetic in content and anointing.

The word "prophetic" here means to pray the Word with revelation, or praying the "rhema" word that comes out of your heart. The anointing that comes from the prophet's office has the ability to confront evil governments, bind strongmen, and set captives free to hear and receive the gospel.

The watchman must have an anointing that enables him to enforce God's laws and protect His work here on the earth. The watchman must be alert, awake, and sober. He must rely on the revelation gifts of the spirit (again, the prophet's anointing) to bring him the information (weapons of warfare) that he needs to carry out his duties.

Above all, the watchman must be knowledgeable of The Word, be one who knows The Word, is committed to meditating on The Word, and have a strong relationship with God through worship, prayer, and personal devotion. The watchman must be filled with the spirit and walk in the spirit at all times.

THE WATCHMAN'S POSITION

"... And the watchman went up to the roof over the gate unto the wall, and lifted up his eyes, and looked ..." 2 Samuel 18:24

Since we are spiritual Israel, A spiritual wall has replaced the natural wall on which the watchman was positioned in the natural nation of Israel. Actually, the watchman was placed in a *high tower on the wall*, from which he could see into the far distance.

He could watch the approaching enemy and accurately discern if the one approaching was friend or foe. He was on the front lines of battle since he saw the enemy first and was first to defend the city. So we New Testament watchmen are positioned in the spirit, and *by virtue of the anointing* that we have received from God, are seated in heavenly places with Christ.

One mistake that is commonly made by believers is to assume that we are all anointed for every job in the Bible, by faith. Nothing could be further from the truth. The anointing of God is something that is conferred by God upon those who not only are called, but who also pay the price. The anointing to rule and reign with him comes through suffering with him. This requires sacrifice. The watchman must pay the price that God demands for the anointing.

The lay watchman must be under watchman's teaching by a senior prophet to receive the anointing. Whether it is by newsletter, book, tape, or conference, e-mail, or regular weekly teaching, the lay (and also the five-fold) watchman must be a person who is *under authority of one who is anointed to do governmental warfare.* As we increase our understanding of the anointing, we find more and more that the anointing for service comes through impartation, both through preaching and the laying on of hands. No longer can we be an army of the Lord without being under proper teaching and authority.

SO YOU WANT TO BE A MARINE?

This is so real it is frightening how many people miss it. If you want to be a Marine, you must join the Marine Corps, (the word "Corps" means "body"), leave you familiar surroundings, submit to all the rigors of training, and then live the lifestyle of a Marine. In order to function as God's Army, we must be trained by those with proven fruit, who demonstrate or carry out that ministry. We must submit as *they* require, pay the price to receive the anointing and then do the works that God has given them to do.

It is unlikely that we can say we are a part of the Marine Corps and not have the credentials: the uniform, papers, training, skills, authority and fruit to show for it. If you carry a certain title, people expect that you can accomplish certain things and have certain abilities significant of that title.

So often Christians miss it through ignorance or arrogance. Ignorance causes us to not seek knowledge and respect authority. Arrogance causes us to assume that we know a thing when we have never been taught. Many people assume they are qualified to minister just because they think they know more scripture than most people in their churches. They don't know that *you must be anointed to do the job you are trying to do.* Many people assume mere words are the same thing as anointed words.

In my experience in the ministry, I have met many people who are grossly mistaken and ignorant concerning how ministry occurs. When you teach a school of ministry as I do, you see many things. Most people want glory for themselves.

They think it's cool to stand before people. When you ask them to take on a more menial, yet highly valued job in the ministry they are upset and insulted. They have "itching hands" and run here and there laying hands on people without the unction, words or anointing.

There was once a lady in our meetings who said that the anointing was on her for healing because her hand shook, but when she went to lay hands on people told me, "you say the words, I don't know what to say." Needless to say, nobody was healed. Healing happens by the words that we speak as well as the anointing.

 *"He sent His Word, and healed them, and delivered them from their destructions." Psalm 107:20*

If the Holy Ghost is moving upon you to lay hands on someone, he will also give you the unction to speak to direct the anointing. This lady left offended, of course, saying that she had learned everything God wanted her to learn in only three short months. It seems that people think of some meetings as "free-for-alls" where you can experiment on the other saints who are there.

People want to lay hands on everybody in the meeting, but they're afraid to witness to their neighbors, they're scared of their families, and if you check, few if any in the families are saved and serving the Lord. Yet they feel they have something to offer the Body of Christ.

AUTOMATICALLY QUALIFIED?

Believers are commanded to lay hands on the sick and cast out devils while preaching the gospel, but it takes study and effort to become a believer. Just because you are born again and speak in tongues does not mean you are automatically qualified to perform every work that believers see in the Bible. You must be taught.

So many people I see have empty, fruitless, and impotent ministries because they lack teaching. One other false notion I see accepted now is that of what some call "mentoring." I've had people I see twice a year say that I am their mentor. "I consider you my mentor," they say. I wait for them to show up at our weekly meetings and they never come. Then when they call, they want me to "cover" them while they do this and "cover" them while they do that.

I asked one such person to come to explain to me their ministry if they expected me to cover them (whatever that means). When they couldn't explain what they did, they were offended at my questions. To this day, I get the old icicle. Mentoring is a relationship and relationship comes with a price.

I remember a story told by the late Brother Lester Sumrall. He has had young ministers come up to him asking for "his mantle." This servant of God could go anywhere in the world, and as Prophet Roberts Liardon says, "When he stepped off the plane, he *owned that part of the world*." What that means is that God had conferred upon Brother Sumrall an anointing that gave him the *authority to rule for the Kingdom of God* in that country.

This governmental anointing is not cheap, nor does it come without paying the price in study, lifestyle, and acquiring knowledge. Anyone, therefore, who wanted what Brother Sumrall had, had to pay the price, mostly through some type of hardship or sacrifice or service. In fact, one of the definitions of *warfare* is *"the apostolic ministry as one of hardship."* Many people think anointings come upon us from others through a one-time trip through a prayer line. The truth is, God sets the price for his anointing, and it always includes discipleship.

Discipleship includes sitting under a senior person and being taught until that person releases you into a ministry. When you are released to minister, you should be able to minister just as that senior person does. Man never controls these things. Being a disciple of that person who carries the anointing you desire to have is the primary means of obtaining it, but there is sacrifice involved here. The disciples forsook all and followed Jesus. They worked with Him and for Him. They lived with Him daily.

We are all disciples of the Lord Jesus Christ. Talking with him about your ministry is the best way to receive instruction, but He will tell you, also, to submit to the teaching of those more experienced and with proven fruit in their ministries. The five-fold are gifts given unto men to teach them to be mature and to teach them the work of the ministry. The prophet who functions as a watchman is uniquely called to teach the ministry of the watchman.

"And he commanded them, saying, This is the thing that ye shall do; A third part of you that enter in on the Sabbath shall even be keepers of the watch of the king's house ... even they shall keep the watch of the house of the Lord about the king."
2 Kings 11:5, 7b

CHAPTER FOUR

The Biblical Functions of the Watchman

Whether the watchman functions at a five-fold or in a lay capacity, his ministry should include the following operations we find by studying watchmen in The Word of God.

DEFENSIVE PROTECTION

The Word of God gives many examples of watchmen playing a vital role in defending the people of God. The building of towers for the purpose of defense is seen with the building of the Tower of Babel (Gen. 11:9).

Although the people who were building were enemies of God, the concept of elevating oneself to a high enough position to set a watch is part of the natural man's wisdom. Thus we see the people of God, natural Israel, using the same methods for protection.

In Judges Chapter 9 we see the story of Gideon's son Abimelech, who wages a civil war against his brethren for control of the Kingdom of Israel. He appears to be successful until he chases all the people of the city to the *stronghold*, or strong tower within the city. The strong tower is a picture of the name of Jesus.

 *"The name of the Lord is a strong tower: the righteous runneth into it, and is safe." Proverbs 18:10*

Where natural Israel ran to a physical high tower, New Testament believers have a spiritual high tower, the name of Jesus as our refuge. As all the people assembled inside the tower, Abimelech set fire to it. Before his destruction could be carried out, a woman threw a millstone down onto Abimelech's head and crushed it, thus defending the people against death. The position of the tower is a vantage point both for protection and for offensive activities.

When we are anointed to do this level of warfare, we are seated in heavenly places with Christ. It is from this position of authority that we aim down at powers that are under the Lord's feet. This is not a position that we assume by faith, but it comes with knowledge and understanding of the tactics of the wicked one. We rule and reign with Him.

REVELATION OR SUPERSTITION?

Obtaining knowledge from God about the strategies of the devil requires careful and through study of The Word of God. Many times we base our knowledge of the enemy on thoughts we receive through a spirit of superstition, not the Holy Spirit's knowledge and wisdom and our understanding of The Word.

For instance, it is commonly said among believers that they are being attacked by the devil because of their call, their work for God, and often they look for signs that God is going to do something wonderful because of the devil's attacks. While this may be true from time to time, it is more coincidence than doctrine. God never uses the devil to point to his glory. In fact when the devils would speak out at Jesus, he would tell them to shut up. We don't need the devil's help to predict what God will do.

Predicting the future in this fashion is known as divination, and is a form of witchcraft. Just because the devil attacks you is no sign that God is going to bless you real big. People who hold to this type of thinking are often making excuses for their lack of power against the devil and their lack of unction to oppose him.

I have observed that these same people never get the great blessing they said was coming because the devil was attacking them. Even worse, few of them ever make much progress in getting the devil under their feet, because they are basing their "revelation," on superstition and emotion instead of The Word of God. Thinking the devil is attacking you because of your great power tends to make you passive toward fighting him, and also will lead you to use your faith to expect some type of trouble. This causes nothing but chaos, and invites familiar spirits to tag along behind you to every meeting you do and every effort you make for God.

The watchman is often called upon to pray in such a way that his prayers are a defense against certain death, both for the people of God and the sinner, as well. God may place a burden to pray upon you at an unexpected time due to a current attack against someone who needs your help. He may have a set watch for you, where you will declare The Word of the Lord to the enemy to keep him bound. Often God will do both. Our prayers of protection are best prayed *before danger gets near and as a routine to keep oppression far from us.*

OFFENSIVE PROTECTION: WARNING

Whenever possible, it is advantageous for the person being protected to *know when he is approaching danger* so that he may avoid it and walk in the wisdom of God where there is protection and safety. The warning function of the watchman allows the person being warned to avoid danger through his own efforts of obedience to God.

 *"Son of man, I have made thee a watchman unto the house of Israel: therefore, hear The Word at my mouth, and give them warning from me." Ezekiel 3:17*

Ezekiel receives further instructions from the Lord. The Lord explains that He will speak to the watchman to give certain messages to the wicked and to the righteous. The watchman is therefore instructed to give the warning to the person *in an effort to save the person's life.* This is something for which prophets may be criticized.

Somehow people, whether righteous or wicked may not want to hear that they are in trouble and need to change. God gives warning to people who are able to repent, that is, to change their minds about the direction in which they are headed. God promises the watchman that if the righteous or wicked repent and not stumble over the stumbling block in their path, they will not die in their sins, and the prophet is not liable for that person's soul. If the prophet fails to warn that person and they die in their sins, the prophet is guilty of that person's blood. (Eze. 33:2-7) Responsibility carries with it a penalty if the duties are not carried out. God is depending on the watchman.

We can see this in the ministry of John the Baptist. John preached the warning to Israel to repent, for the Kingdom of Heaven was at hand. God sent the stumbling stone, Jesus, into the earth to bring the Kingdom. Many Jews stumbled at this, but because John had warned them, his hands were innocent of the blood of the nation of Israel.

The lay watchman may function in this warning capacity, also. Parents may need to warn their children to get back on the path of righteousness. When teenagers keep the wrong company, we may find through prayer that they are being set up by the enemy for some type of failure. It is good to know that as you are faithful in carrying out your duties as a watchman to warn of impending danger, you can save a soul. Remember that God holds the watchman accountable for The Words that he gives him.

 *"I will stand upon my watch, and set me upon the tower, and will watch to see what he will say unto me, and what I shall answer when I am reproved." Habakkuk 2:1*

OBSERVATION

The watchman functions much like the security guard or night watchman in this role. Much of what watchmen observe is non-threatening. The mere presence of the watchman scatters evil. Just as a uniformed policeman commands respect, so the anointing of the watchman demands respect in the spirit. The spiritual eyes of the watchman cause a certain degree of response by principalities. Often people say of prophets, "I feel like they can see right through me."

This seeing eye is more of an observational look than anything else. It is impossible for the watchman to lose the seeing eye or the listening ear. Look at Samson, who never developed his prophetic abilities to see in the spirit. Eventually his eyes were plucked out (Judges 16:21). What you use for God will be preserved.

The watchman relies upon the Holy Spirit to tell him what he sees. If God doesn't tell you it's there, it is not there. Some people may begin to develop this ability to see in the spirit, and if they are not trained and disciplined, they will think everything that moves has to be bound and talked about for years. Sometimes the devil is involved but there is no unction from God to move against him. God's timing is perfect. We all need training and discipline. Remember little Samuel who started out not even knowing that it was God speaking to him (1 Samuel 3:3-10)?

Later, after God trained him under Eli the priest, he heard from God so accurately that God let none of his words fall to the ground (1 Samuel 3:19).

The prophet was in old times known as a seer (1 Samuel 9:9) because God spoke to the seer in visions and dreams. The prophet today has the same ability. Gifts of God do not change, only the administration of the gift varies because of the New Covenant.

Prophets and watchmen must have the ability to observe by focusing their attention toward God at all times. This is not a "put on" thing, but is a real sensitivity or alertness to God's stirring to get their attention. If you are a prophet and not given to visions and dreams, you can still observe by the spirit. This ability to observe is far more valuable than visions and dreams, because it can come upon you quickly and you can move accurately in prayer when your senses are tuned into God.

The ability to discern with spiritual senses is a "must have" for the watchman, and God will develop this in you.

BRING DIVINE REVELATION

The revelation gifts of the Holy Spirit operate in a very strong and consistent manner through the prophet's office. The prophet, functioning as a watchman, is capable of receiving revelation in a greater measure than are the other ministry gift offices. John the Divine received the remarkable visions that we see reported in the book of the Revelation. Peter fell into a trance in which the Lord spoke to him and let him know that the gospel is for all men (Acts 10:10 ff). The prophet Elisha was allowed to hear the battle plans of the Syrian army through the gift of The Word of knowledge (1 Kings 6:12).

The natural watchmen of the nation of Israel were able to watch from their high towers and discern who was approaching. They knew if the person was friend or foe. They could also discern where the person came from and report to the King what they observed (2 Samuel 18:24-27). The watchman was responsible for reporting what he saw to the appropriate person. His job is incomplete until the information he gathers goes to the right person.

As the watchman reports to the Lord what he sees, the Lord may tell him to continue to pray, but he may also tell the watchman to report to a superior what he sees. It is common for watchmen to share what God reveals to them to other watchmen or to the leader who oversees the company of watchmen.

If it is indeed Divine revelation, the information can be incorporated in the prayers of the watchmen. If it is not Divine revelation, it must be discarded or put on the shelf until God explains or tells the leader what to do with the information. Divine revelation is always useful. Information gathered through suspicion or gossip will not have the results of God, and must be avoided. Judge by the spirit through which the information is given, and also whether the information is consistent with God's patterns as set forth in His word.

WARFARE

"Just do it," says the Nike[1] slogan. The Lord gave these words to me to describe how I would train the people who came to learn this ministry. I was to put the prayer manual into their hands and tell them to "just do it." Just pray the prayers and let the anointing of God do the rest of the work. That's just how simple warfare is, but you must have accurate information, the right weapons, and of course,

---

[1] Greek word for victory.

the anointing. Since the prayers came from the Divine revelation of God, when they are prayed in faith the anointing is there. God allowed me to see that this simple form of submission to instruction would allow anyone who followed the simple directions concerning the use of our prayer manuals to receive the anointing that is on this ministry as far as the prayers are concerned. Many people have reported great success using our prayer manuals.

One of my favorite accounts of the watchman's warfare is the account of Elijah facing Jezebel and the prophets of Baal at Matthew Carmel (2 Ki. 18:8). The prophet as watchman is called *to confront evil spiritual governments.* His weapons are not carnal, but mighty through God.

That day on Matthew Carmel, Elijah had a showdown that allowed the evil to be exposed, and the people of Israel were set free. It seems that God merely wants truth established in the earth, and the people then are free to decide what they desire.

Elijah knew that his God was the Most High God, but in order to get that established among the people, he had to *confront* and *dethrone* the god, Baal. He also had to confront the leaders of his own people. The watchman is often called to pray through in critical issues like this.

In the end, Elijah established that his God was the most powerful. One of the results of the prayers of the watchman is that they will result in a greater manifestation of the power of God. That is why this ministry is being reestablished in a greater capacity in this hour. If we want to usher in the second coming of the Lord, there must be an increase of His glory in the earth. He will be coming for a glorious church because He is the Lord of Glory. The watchman is playing a vital role in the advent of the Bridegroom toward His Bride.

ANOTHER GREAT WARRIOR OF OUR TIME

One of my favorite contemporary church leaders is Dr. Martin Luther King. I draw a great deal of wisdom and insight from reading his writings. He too was a watchman. By confronting the spirit of racism, he was able to see many people set free by the hand of the Lord. He relied heavily upon The Word of the Lord. He had diligently studied the scriptures, and seemed to be thrust into the leadership role of the desegregation movement when a seamstress who said she was merely "tired from working all day, and wanted to sit down on the bus," refused to stand while there were empty seats on the bus.

Of course, the empty seats were in the "white section" of the bus, but this act of boldness on the part of Rosa Parks was the spark that ignited the civil rights movement of the 1960's. The ideologies of the Prince of this world are all absurd, just as racism is absurd. Children growing up in this present generation sometimes find it hard to believe that laws that made it illegal for blacks to sit at a lunch counter next to a white person, or to use the same drinking fountain or restroom were ever enacted in this country, but they were, and vestiges of the spirit of racism still control people's minds.

Look at the skinhead and white supremacist movements. The devil is constantly birthing new strategies to keep the people confused, in strife, and away from the blessings that come with keeping the God's commandment to love one another. (John 13:34)

Many politicians and knowledgeable people had told Dr. King that it was not the right time to address the issue of race, *but Dr. King heard a different voice.* I'm sure the children of Israel felt that it was not the right time to leave Egypt, even after they were gone they felt this way, but those who have the eyes of the prophet see otherwise. They make their minds up by the voice of God. Whenever God wants to make a change, he makes it. He does not care that the political climate is contrary to what He decides to do.

Because of Dr. King's prayers, activities, and stand to confront the wickedness of racism, we as a nation enjoy greater blessings. Dr. King is not alive to enjoy these blessings, but we see them every day. After the civil rights and voting rights acts of the 1960's, the economy of the south was revived. Many industries shut down their northern facilities to head south. Governor George Wallace of Alabama publicly repented of his wrong ideas.

Only God can change a person's heart and cause the blind to see. This type of fruit is the type seen in spiritual revival. People turn away from their damning ideas and turn back to God. Was there a revival in the 1960's? You'd better believe there was. Because one man chose to lead the warfare against racism, many young people of both races were born again.

The Jesus Movement of the 1960's was marked by the theme of brotherly love, with the end of racial prejudice. We finally saw blacks and whites working together, living in the same neighborhoods, and respecting one another. This attitude continues to this day.

When the strongman who controls an ideology or mindset is defeated, then God's spirit can move on the hearts of people. They see the light and come to repentance over their wicked ways.

But watchmen have to continue to beat the spirit of racism and prejudice until it is completely dead. Our churches have a long way to go. It is said that 11 a.m. Sunday is the most segregated hour of the week. Churches have to kill racism on purpose. We must make a deliberate effort to integrate our churches and ministries. We are to set an example for the world of brotherly love.

Watchmen of this present age must stand on their guard to declare to the evil prince of racism that we will not be moved. We are going forward to greater glory, so we continue to bind and confront the Spirit of racism in our prayers. We pray until the enemy is completely subdued.

EXECUTING WRITTEN JUDGMENTS: CARRYING OUT THE WORD OF THE LORD

Jesus defeated Satan with the three words, "it is written" (Luke 4). Then He spoke the scripture to the devil, who left him alone for a season. Our weapon of warfare is The Word of God. We execute written judgment upon the devil by using The Word of the Lord.

When we say "Word of the Lord," it refers to a word spoken to our hearts by the Holy Spirit that is fitting for that situation, not just any scripture we may think of.

It is important for us to remember that Jesus did everything by *unction of the Spirit*. This is how to get results from God. Not knowing the unction of the Spirit will cost us dearly. Often we do not train ourselves to obey the unction. We often say, "I didn't feel led," meaning we did not obey the unction to move on something when it is obvious that God wanted us to move. Or we do things by impulse and call it unction. Self-condemnation and self-doubt will keep us in confusion about what to do. Whenever we move in the spirit, the Holy Ghost's leading must be there if we are to get the results of God.

Everything God wants us to do is written in his word. We can execute judgment on pornography, child abuse, incest, theft, lying, divorce, deceit, adultery, witchcraft, and all evil because it is written that they are sin and an abomination to God. His word is His judgment.

Whatever God has spoken against is already judged. So what are we here doing? Since we have dominion on the earth, whatever we allow is allowed, and whatever we disallow is disallowed (Matthew 16:19; 18:18).

If we do not want guns brought to our schools, we need to pray a hedge of thorns around our schools and the children in them. This keeps the devil out and God's will in. When we tell the devil, "thou shalt not kill," we are executing written judgment against him. The word of the Lord is being carried out; the strong carry out His word.

When we get an assignment from God to *pray* for something, we must remember that we take a stand *against* certain evils. Whenever an assault is made against the devil, he will strike back, or regroup his forces to form a counter strategy.

People who do not understand and accept this will assume that because things appear to be worse for a season that they are not going to win. But I've got good news. We have already won. We only need to continue to wrestle away the devil's prey. It may be a sick child, a depressed loved one, or financial problems, but "it is written." The devil is defeated and Jesus is Lord of all and has redeemed us from the devil's power.

THE CASE AGAINST ASSISTED SUICIDE

We moved to Detroit seven years ago. When I first heard of Jack Kevorkian, I thought, "you know, we've really deteriorated as a society. I can't believe they're allowing this man to actually kill people and they do nothing about it." The "they" who need to do something about any evil is always the church. I began praying that God would intervene. Of course, all the watchmen in our ministry pray for the same concerns.

So here we are, twenty-five or so people praying for this evil to stop and it gets worse. I have begun praying with many people for many things. Some people continue, but many drop out when the prayer is not answered in three months. How would you like to wrestle the devil for ten years?

Communism in Russia was fought for seventy years. The reason they call him a strong man is just that—he's strong. And he has supporters. Every person who supports his wicked ideas is a hindrance to others receiving the truth. But we have one stronger than the strongman living in us. It is in Him that we live and move and have our being.

After three years praying in Cleveland with poor results, I find myself in Detroit. One year is spent in oblivion wondering what a nice girl like me is doing here. But I begin to observe, and get the lay of the land.

After a year, I begin the call in the spirit for the watchmen to show up. I visit all kinds of prophetic churches and prayer groups and find all kinds of prayer, but no true watchmen. "I will have to make them," I decide. This is always true for an apostle or prophet who begins a work. You cannot build on another man's foundation (Romans 15:20).

After one year, I find two people living in Canada who seem to desire to know this ministry. One of them provides a place for our meeting. Of course we're fought in every way, but we prevail.

Along the way, I learn the identity of the strongman over the city of Detroit. I know how he supports the idea of assisted suicide. I begin to obtain the strategy from God for his demise. It will not be a snap. I first have to train the watchmen to The Word of God. We have to believe nothing but The Word of God. Some are offended at correction and leave. People come to meetings with all kinds of pre-conceived ideas. Some think this will be a free for all of laying hands on one another and giving "words" to one another, but it is not. Some will have to decide if it is worth the trouble, but we continue to build the ministry.

It is very important not to try to be a "Lone Ranger," or proceed without wisdom in training others to the ministry. Every person God sends is important to the success of your ministry. Don't overlook the importance of people. Don't ever think you can take a city alone.

As we begin to pray with the new strategy, we see Jack Kevorkian, who in his reign of terror, kill at least 30 people, mock the courts and dare them to file charges against him. The prosecutor seems intimidated. People begin to confess that the prosecutor will never get a conviction. Even the prosecutor agrees. This is part of the devil's armament. He bombards us with the evil report. He mocks and taunts to see if he can intimidate us into backing down and in so doing, allow him to continue his evil. Then Satan allows those that he uses to fall by The Word of the Lord because that is exactly what happened.

In April of 1999, Jack Kevorkian was found guilty of murder. This is because the watchmen executed The Word of the Lord and did not quit or become distracted by another ministry they "felt led" to do. True watchmen accept this call as a life's work. Twenty years from now, you will find us doing the same thing.

Because of the lawlessness that is promoted by the strongman in this area, people were intimidated by Jack Kevorkian's taunts, and even compromised on the law. Many news commentators hailed him as a hero, saying he was way ahead of his time, and that in years to come, people will recognize what a genius he was.

My prayer is that the remembrance of him be removed from the minds of people. We curse the works of darkness and their fruit. I wondered from time to time if we would ever see an end to his works, but God began to turn the tide in 1998.

That year God showed me a vision of what would become of the city of Detroit if this evil were not stopped. I saw lines of traffic backed up on all the major freeways. People were bringing the sick to be put to death. Factories were turned into crematoriums and cemeteries, as the industry changed to accommodate the new laws.

The word of the Lord to me was, "you must stop this evil while it is in the birthing stages or this will be a town given over to death. It will be impossible to have a move of God in this type of atmosphere. I want this man tried and convicted of murder."

At first I wanted to pray for Jack to die, but I heard God say, "that would do little good. I want to expose him to the world as evil, so the hearts and minds of the people will be changed. The people must learn again to hate killing for any reason."

Now you understand why this city had been dubbed the murder capital of the world. The spirit of lawlessness carries with it a strong spirit of destruction, death, and murder. Prayer to change the hearts and minds of people takes longer. Killing the perpetrator is a quick solution, but it does little to change ideas. In fact, the devil would love to martyr someone like him. People would make a cult hero out of him, instead of bringing him to shame.

Jack Kevorkian is sentenced to spend his remaining ears behind bars. He has been ordered to pay the state room and board costs for his prison stay. Any money he has or has coming will go to the state. Many of the people who once supported him cannot be heard of now.

A growing counter movement has begun bringing together Christians, the elderly and infirm to fight these laws allowing assisted suicide. The law in Oregon that passed has yet to be carried out. People suddenly seem to not be so interested in executing their rights to "death with dignity."

Another strategy of the devil in building mental strongholds is to change terminology to acceptable and less threatening sounding words. This movement to make everything "politically correct" is a strategy that works to help people to accept the unacceptable. Words like "assisted suicide," "death with dignity," "right to choose," are coined to take the place of "murder." When we use subtlety, guile, or deceit, we are operating in witchcraft. Often what we call "tact" is simply an attempt to beguile someone into accepting our way.

The Word of the Lord, when executed, will bring about dramatic results. I remember talking to intercessors about Jack Kevorkian. When he was arrested, few made any comment about his arrest. A sure sign they had quit praying long ago. Watchmen cannot afford to quit. When God gives assignments, He does so to people He knows will bring back the heads of the uncircumcised Philistines.

ESTABLISHING DIVINE ORDER IN THE CHURCH

The prayers of the watchman bring Divine order into the church. One of the assignments we have had since we began this ministry is to see the fulfillment of Eph. 4:11. This was one of the first scriptures the Lord gave me to establish as a foundation of the ministry. He did this both to explain my function in the Body of Christ and also to give direction to our prayers. God wants to raise up many mature sons and daughters. One of the scriptures in the Song of Solomon, the bridal call, speaks of an immature young girl who is waiting to be betrothed,

"We have a little sister, and she hath no breasts: what shall we do for our sister in the day when she shall be spoken for?" Song of Solomon 8:8

The little sister, of course is the immature bride, the one who cannot give birth or nourishment. When the Lord empowers the bride, then she will be able to reproduce and bear fruit for the Lord. Her maturity comes with the ministry of the five-fold ministry gifts, all of them. There is a purpose for every ministry gift in our lives. If we wish to mature, we have to come out of hiding and get into the light. We have to quit seeing the church as a place to attend out of habit or routine merely to get rid of guilt, and see it instead as a vibrant, living organism that gives us life, and enables and empowers us in turn to give life to others.

So we pray for the setting in order of the five-fold ministry gifts to govern the church. We also pray against the release of immature or false gifts, something that happens often. The role of the gift of prophecy is so important here.

Just as Samuel was able to see gifts in all of Jesse's children (1 Samuel 16:1-13), so the prophet today is able to "see" by the Spirit the gifts, callings, and proper placement of the parts of the body of Christ. This setting of Divine order allows people to make right choices concerning their church affiliation, and teaching and training regarding their ministry. The gift of prophecy allows a settling in of the will of God in a person, and keeps his vision clear regarding his place in the body.

PREPARING THE WAY OF THE LORD

John the Baptist had a wonderful ministry. Jesus called him "more than a prophet." But John said of himself in comparison to Jesus, "I must decrease, and He must increase" (John 3:30). The watchman, if he is to increase in power, must decrease in himself. The longer he works for God, the more he is given over to the work of the ministry, until finally the way of the Lord is properly prepared.

When we prepare the way of the Lord, we preach repentance, submission to the ways of God, worship, and prayer. We admonish and encourage the people to "get serious" about God. We call people back to sobriety. Sometimes people are distracted by problems, or they may begin to gravitate to certain popular teachings that leave them imbalanced in their knowledge.

Often, people have walked away from the basics of the gospel: praying for the salvation of family and loved ones, and praying for the needs of the family, friends, and co-workers. Often during stagnant times the work of the gospel among the poor and disadvantaged is neglected. We become interested in larger buildings, instead of enlarging the hearts of the people to reach out to the poor.

God draws the watchman's attention to these things, and he begins to pray, preach, and declare and war. The prophet's ministry is often one of confrontation of evil, distraction, worldliness, and wickedness. The watchman hates selfishness, and recoils when he sees it in himself as well as others. The watchman must be willing to live under God's microscope, and confront wrong attitudes in any anyone that God points to.

For instance, when John the Baptist preached repentance, he told the people what sins they were guilty of and needed to turn away from. For the soldier it was being dissatisfied with his wages, for the lawyer, it was being dishonest in his dealings, for Herod, it was marrying his sister-in-law, who had a living husband.

This cost him his head, but he preached it, anyway. Does the watchman live on the edge? You'd better believe it, but there is no other ministry that will get this particular job done, and it must be done if Jesus is going to return and receive a mature, perfected bride. Jesus is coming for a bride equipped to rule and reign with Him during the Millennium.

 "For thus hath the Lord said unto me, Go, set a watchman, let him declare what he seeth...And he cried, A lion: My lord, I stand continually upon the watchtower in the daytime, and I am set in my ward whole nights." Isaiah 21:6, 8

CHAPTER FIVE

The Vision of the Watchman:
The Lighthouse as a Symbol

I don't remember exactly when it started, but the Lord began to speak to me about the purpose of this ministry and made references to the lighthouse. Many prayer ministries used the warrior symbol, or praying hands, but we have used the lighthouse, because it speaks more to the specific work and vision of the watchman. The position of the lighthouse speaks to the vantage position of the watchman. The typical lighthouse was placed in a high vantage point in the middle of the darkness of the ocean.

The placement of the lighthouse was very strategic. The *lighthouse* was placed in a precarious position. The more dangerous the place, the more the lighthouse is needed. If there is a place where the gospel flows freely and everybody is saved, healed and delivered, there is enough light there already for safe navigation. However, in uncharted territory, territory where not much of the power of God flows, or territory with many unseen and hidden dangers, there is more need for the lighthouse and the vision of the watchman.

The vision of the watchman is also needed in times when all is going well to maintain, sustain, and protect what is established. To give an example, there have been many "revivals," in the history of the world. Most revivals begin with prayer, waiting upon God, and a response from God to the people.

There is a revelation on God's Word released in every revival, with the resultant fruit or evidence of that truth among the people. A good example is Martin Luther's Protestant Revolution of the sixteenth century in which Luther protested the sale of salvation through indulgences, a practice common in the Catholic Church. Luther heard from God that "the just shall live by faith." This led to the doctrine of salvation by grace through faith available to all.

This was revolutionary for the time, but our current teaching on the "word of faith" is a result of that simple revelation. Once scripture is brought to light, it keeps reproducing truth. The watchman's work is to protect the availability of revealed truth.

However, there is always an opposing force that will refute the truth. This is where the ministry of the watchman is necessary to initiate the release of current truth and defy the forces of darkness that would steal, pollute, or pervert that truth. The watchman must be on guard for the leaven of the Pharisees that is injected into The Word of God to puff it up and make it of none effect. The watchman must also be aware that religion will come to make light of the revelation so that people do not hold fast to it, or will magnify that revelation to the point that none of the other truths of God's Word necessary to support that truth can be heard.

The watchman is the keeper of the light. Jesus was a watchman. He walked out upon the water in the fourth watch of the night when his disciples were in trouble of drowning (Matthew 14:25) and rescued them. When He was with them asleep in the bottom of the ship, He was their safety and security (Luke 8:22-24). It's good to know that He is the Chief Watchman. A good watchman knows when to be awake, and when to sleep.

When the watchman appears, he brings light with him. Just as the light of the lighthouse guided the ships to safety, so the revelation of The Word of God spoken and prayed by the watchman provides guidance and safety to the Body of Christ. Light chases darkness and causes it to flee.

The light that the watchman brings protects life just as a lifeboat that brings rescued people safely to shore. The Word of God is our ark of safety or vehicle that takes us to our destinations in the spirit. The watchman, then is the light (because of Christ in him), and is the keeper of the light. We are the temple of God, so we are a lighthouse. As we go forth declaring the Word of the Lord, we bring light, hope, and safety to a world in darkness.

A BRIEF LIGHTHOUSE HISTORY

The lighthouse came into existence because of necessity. Is the ministry of the watchman a necessity to the Kingdom of God? You be the judge.

As we examine the similarities between the function of the watchman in the Kingdom of God and the functions of the lighthouse to help those who travel the seas, we will see that the concept of watching, warning and protection have been and perhaps always will be a very necessary part of life on earth as we know it.

Lighthouses became useful to sailors who frequently sailed the seas because they were landmarks to alert them to their location. They were a source of direction, safety, and comfort to sailors. During the night, the open seas are very dark. So dark, that often, the sailor could not see his hand before his face. When navigating close to shore, it was impossible to see if one were close to the rocks, or if there were dangerous underwater shoals[†] that would cause the boat to be grounded. Often the navigator would not know how close to shore he was, so the lighthouse gave a flood of light over the otherwise black sea.

What a blessing it was when the captain of the ship saw that beacon of light guiding him safely to shore. The prayers of the watchman provide such a beacon. Our prayers can cover a wide territory or they can give light, safety, and peace in your own home. Modern lighthouses can project light as far as eighteen miles away, offering a broad ray of hope to the otherwise sightless navigator.

Many lighthouses were built after shipwrecks. Fed up with losing precious cargo, mariners sought a means to help them guide their ships safely to shore. Many times in our walk with God, we may find that we have smooth sailing

---

[†] Shoals are sandy elevations at the sea bottom that cause navigational hazards.

up to a point, and then the way gets rocky. This indicates our need for the vision of the watchman. The watchman sees danger, and can cause us to avoid shipwreck by warning us of things to come and also interceding for God's mercy and grace. Mercy allows us to ride out the rough spots. Grace enables us to continue on course and reach our destination.

THE FIRST LIGHTHOUSE

The first lighthouse recorded in history was considered one of the Seven Wonders of the World. It was the Pharos of Alexandria located on the bank of the Hellespont, the body of water that separated ancient Greece from Turkey. It was commissioned by Ptolemy II, King of Egypt to "serve every man who voyages in a boat."

Did you know that the prayers of the watchman benefit the sinner as well as the saint? Whenever God moves, He does exceeding and abundantly above all that we can ask or think. One of the redemptive names of our God is "El Shaddai" the God who is more than enough or the God who brings the overflow.

Whenever you pray for a need as a Christian, understand that the world will be blessed by your overflow. You cannot contain the great blessing that God will bring to you when you pray His Word.

The Pharos of Alexandria was located on the Isle of Pharos in the bay of Alexandria on the Mediterranean Sea. Thousands of slaves did the work of building this huge monument. It took twenty years to be completed, was constructed of white marble, and stood four hundred feet from the middle of a huge courtyard surrounded by galleries that contained rare artwork.

This three-story structure housed hundreds of workmen who kept the wood-burning flame atop the structure ablaze during the night. It was said that this flame was visible for thirty miles.

Above the brazier that housed the flame was a statue of the Greek god of the sea, Poseidon, with his trident in one hand. It is said that his other hand held a mirror so clear that enemy ships could be seen in it over one hundred leagues away. So spectacular was this lighthouse that every lighthouse built after that was called a "pharos."

The Pharos of Alexandria lasted 1600 years, from about 250 B.C. to about 1349. It was found in ruins and no one knows to this day if it was destroyed by Turks, an earthquake, or some mysterious power.

The next "lighthouse" or light structure known to be built was the Colossus of Rhodes, built by the Greeks. It was actually a bronze statue of a man straddling a narrow inlet off the harbor of Rhodes. Little is known of it, no pictures or much data about it exists. It is just reported to have been a light structure of the Greek sun god, Helios.

Next, the Romans built Caligula's light in 40 A.D. Located off the coast of France (then Gaul) it was to mark the site of the Roman's encampment. At one time, Rome ruled the entire known world. When Henry VIII of England captured Boulogne in 1544, he converted this lighthouse to a fort by building four bastions and a wall around it. After 1644 it was never used as a lighthouse again.

In Europe, many lighthouses existed during the time of the Roman Empire because the Romans were master builders. They erected lighthouses wherever they went, and they were plentiful across Europe, and the Middle East. When the Roman Empire collapsed, all of its lighthouses fell into disrepair.

The last ancient lighthouse, the Tower of Hercules off the cost at La Corunna, Spain is probably still in existence. Though not now in operation as a lighthouse, it was during the disaster of the Spanish Armada in 1588, and was used as a landmark for the allies who sailed from England to Normandy in 1944.

THE MOST FAMOUS LIGHTHOUSE IN THE WORLD

The most famous lighthouse ever built was Eddystone Light, first built in 1700. This lighthouse is famous because of the character of its several builders, and because of the dangers through which it was built. Previous lighthouses were built in "safe" areas: inlets off harbors or the inland coast.

Eddystone Light was the first lighthouse built for danger, in danger, and to help persons escape danger. It provided light in the dangerous and reef filled Plymouth Harbor off the coast of England and was actually set on top of one of these reefs. The Mayflower, which came to America in 1620, "barely escaped the reefs in Plymouth harbor," the captain wrote. Many vessels were wrecked in this dangerous place. The English government decided that greater safety was needed, so the first Eddystone Lighthouse was commissioned.

Built by Henry Winstanley in 1700, the first light was a "wonder," to say the least. Mr. Winstanley was a showman and inventor, so the first light contained a bit of his whimsy. He predicted that it would last forever. It functioned for three years, though most of the ornamental work was lost in high winds during the winters.

Fortunately, the watchmen kept the light and no ships were lost during that period. Then in 1703, the worst storm ever hit the English coast. For two weeks, gale force winds hit the lighthouse. Winstanley rushed out to check the tower, and before he could get back to shore, the storm struck again.

It is said that this storm that wrecked over one hundred ships, killed eight thousand sailors, flooded most of England, drowned cattle, and caused roofs to be lifted off homes from miles around, was mocked by Mr. Winstanley, who is said to have shaken his fist at the wind, and said, "come on, test my lighthouse."

This it did. The morning after the storm, nothing was left of Mr. Winstanley or his lighthouse, or its keepers.

The second builder of Eddystone Light was John Rudyerd in 1709. His tower was built in the same place as Winstanley's, and he was careful not to make the same mistakes. He built a cylindrical structure of unbroken lines, where the previous one was eight-sided. The tower was there until 1755 when a fire broke out.

The three keepers hauled water until the fire was out, but left the lighthouse unattended (a breach of lighthouse command) because one of them had swallowed a piece of molten lead. The keepers had no choice but to escape to a neighboring rock and wait for a rescue boat.

One year later in 1756 a young man by the name of John Smeaton built the next Eddysone light. Keep in mind that these lighthouses were built on what amounts to huge rocks in the middle of a rock infested ocean inlet. They had to be placed where they could do the best job of protecting the ships carrying precious cargo.

Building had to be done at low tide, and water had to be pumped off the reef during the building. Smeaton's tower was round and smooth like Rudyerd's, but higher and with the tapered shape that we see in tower lighthouses now. Smeaton was not a showman, but as the son of very successful and tolerant lawyer, he was allowed to study anything in which he had an interest.

He studied building, architecture, bricklaying, and plumbing. He brought hope and confidence to the job of building the lighthouse. It is no wonder that at the age of thirty-two and already a presenter at the Royal Society of London, John Smeaton confidently undertook the building of the third Eddystone Light.

Smeaton's lighthouse took three years to complete. He made many major improvements over the old lighthouses.

Built entirely of granite, its base was far wider and heavier than the previous two, thus giving it a more sure foundation. It's stones interlocked, so that each joint supported the other, and it was more like one piece of stone. It tapered at the top, causing it to circumvent the wind and waves instead of opposing them.

During the years of its building, *no man lost his life, and no man had been severely injured.* Every man was paid generously for his work, and was given extra wages for each hour spent on the rock itself, where he worked soaking wet and miserable. Any man who failed his duty was immediately dismissed. Smeaton's workmen respected and admired him. At the completion of his lighthouse, Smeaton refused to have his name engraved on the stone, which most builders customarily did. Instead he had this inscription from Psalm 127 inscribed. It reads:

"UNLESS THE LORD BUILD THE HOUSE,
THEY LABOR IN VAIN WHO BUILD IT."

We know the second part of that verse:

 *"Unless the Lord keep the city, the watchman waketh in vain." Psalm 127:1*

John Smeaton closed the building by having the final inscription on the cornerstone, "Laus Deo," Latin for "Praise God." His Eddystone Light was in use until 1878, and was rebuilt due to a crumbling foundation. The citizens of Plymouth had it dismantled and re-erected in the town where everyone could see it, and it remains there to this day. The final Eddystone light was built on a different site on the same rock, and due to improvements in technology was taller and more secure than Smeaton's.

WHAT CAN WE LEARN FROM THIS?

We must not miss the revelation in this history of Eddystone Lighthouse. The most successful house was built with a broader and more secure foundation. If you are a watchman, your foundation is The Word of God. The more word you have hidden in your heart and the more Word you pray, the stronger and more fruitful your prayers will be.

Second, Smeaton's lighthouse was built with interlocking stones. We as lively stones in the Lord's lighthouse must work together in corporate fashion to get the results God wants. We must also not seclude ourselves with our "private" revelations between God and us. We must be willing to submit ourselves to the teaching of those God would show us as being elders or "generals" in His army. We must be fitly joined together as a body.

Third, the tower tapered toward the top. As you reach the head, Christ Jesus, there are fewer and fewer people able to hold that position. In other words, the revelation needed to lead this type of warfare will not be "common knowledge" like the knowledge of salvation, or even the baptism in the Holy Spirit. The ability to lead God's army is given to those submitted to Jesus as the head of the church, and built upon the foundation of the doctrine of the apostles and prophets.

Lastly, Mr. Smeaton gave honor and glory to God. The humility needed to carry this ministry cannot be overestimated. To whom much is given, much is required. God demands that we bow down to Him, and not take any credit ourselves.

With each new building, something is taken from the old, and something new is added. That's progress. The fourth light was no exception. Built in 1882 by Sir James Douglas, the fourth Eddystone Light, a 9-story, 140 foot stone tower, with a huge 7-ton oil-burning lantern on top, was much like that of Smeaton. It remains untouched by wind or sea until this day, a tribute to man's perseverance and God's grace.

Douglass, a Godly man who admired John Smeaton, chose also not to have his name inscribed on the lighthouse, but inscribed Psalm 127:1, *"unless the Lord build the house, they labor in vain who build it.* Praise God."

THE LIGHTING OF THE LIGHTHOUSE

All of the building is meaningless unless the lantern provides adequate lighting. The first lights consisted of wood fires kept in metal pans, as in the Pharos of Alexandria. Later coal was used. The obvious disadvantage here is that the keepers of the lights had to frequently carry fuel up to the tower and tend the fire. Smoke and soot require constant cleaning of the instruments and was messy.

Soon these were replaced with the household candle, and these were housed in panes of glass and giant lanterns were created expressly for use in lighthouses. The keeper's primary function with this type of light was to keep the wicks trimmed, thus the term "wickies" was used for one who kept the wicks trimmed.

With the advent of oil as a fuel, candles were replaced. The invention of the circular wick by a Swiss scientist, Ami Argand made the job of trimming much easier. Reflectors were introduced in the early nineteenth century that allowed the light to be seen at a much farther distance.

In most recent times, of course electricity and even automated lighthouses have replaced the older methods. The first electrically powered lighthouse seems to have been our own Statue of Liberty in New York Harbor.

One major advancement in lighting was the invention in 1822 by a French engineer by the name of Augustin Fresnel. He constructed a lens composed of glass prisms ringed around a spherical lens. This Fresnel (*pronounced* Fre nel) lens revolutionized the lighthouse industry, and in no time, most lighthouses had one of the huge lenses. This lens stood ten feet high and six feet wide, and could only be looked at during daylight. The keepers had to polish and clean the lens during the day. At night the light was so bright one could not look directly into it.

The Fresnel lens came in six different sizes, called orders. They ranged in size from the largest, or first order lens, which was about six feet in diameter and visible up to eighteen inches to the sixth order lenses were about 18 inches in diameter, visible to six miles. Flashes of light characterize the identity of the lighthouse by night, color of the lighthouse itself, characterizes the identity of the lighthouse for day; this is called the day mark or day signal. Typical markings may be horizontal stripes, barber pole, or squares.

The movement of the lens is characterized as fixed, which sends out light in 360 degrees, rotating or flashing. The glass of the lens itself has bull's eyes and prisms through which a beam flashes every few seconds. By the variation of flashes, direction and rotations of the light, the mariner always has light, and will get a characteristic light signal that tells him which light is beaming at him if he is in an area where several lights are located.

This is a necessity in areas like the English Channel where there are more than a dozen lights, or the North Atlantic off the coast of Newfoundland, where several lights are located in close proximity to one another. The mariner knows location and can see the way with this type of light.

The watchman, just like the Keeper of the light, must work in the light and respect the light. The light is the Word of God. He must be filled with God's Word in order to be full of light. He also must have such a solid relationship with the Holy Spirit that he knows and understands what operations of the spirit are needed at certain times.

Do we pray in tongues, travail, prophesy, declare, war in dance, shout, groan? All of these operations of the spirit have their perfect place in the ministry of the watchman. When to do each is determined by the moving of the Spirit of God.

There is no room for "pet" maneuvers or counterfeiting something we heard about in the latest seminar. There is no substitute for relationship with God in this ministry.

THE VOICE OF THE LIGHTHOUSE

Even with all these advancements in lighting, there are times when there is not enough visibility for light to help direct a ship. Fog is one of the most dangerous weather hazards facing mariners. The foghorn was developed to guide ships when the fog brought the visibility very low. First cannons were used, with little success.

Bells were used next. One was installed at West Quoddy Head Light in Boston Harbor, a place of frequently dense fog. The bell produced some sound, but could not be heard very far. After the bells, then sirens were tried. Fog boats, moored at various danger points all along the coast were tried, but because their sound was not distinguishable by distance, many of them were wrecked by ships coming too close to them.

With the invention of the radio wave, and later radar, and the short wave, the problem of maritime meteorology seems to have been solved. In this country the coast guard service has taken over the care of lighthouses, and they use radar and radios in vessels to warn of impending danger.

They have also taken over the rescue functions of the lighthouse, a job that the keeper could not easily handle for fear of losing the light. If something happened to the lighthouse keeper during a failed rescue attempt, many more lives may have been lost because of his failure to be upon his watch, keeping the light.

THE RULE OF THE LIGHTHOUSE

This rule of the lighthouse is something of extreme importance both to the natural lighthouse and to the spiritual lighthouse. The primary job of the watchman is to provide light. He is the keeper of the Lord's lighthouse.

If this light were to be extinguished due to failure of the watchman to keep his watch, the lighthouse ceased to function, does not do its job, and many of those who depend upon the light (the prayers of the watchman) would not receive their blessing, or worse, they will perish in the darkness. It is essential that the watch be kept.

The watchman must keep his prayer time with God, must keep his word to his prayer partner, and must always do his job with diligence and zeal. He must live a holy life, keeping his heart pure with all diligence. He cannot be angry or unforgiving. He must keep the command to love, knowing that at any time danger may be lurking, and his prayers are needed. He must be ready to aid and rescue at a moment's notice. He must walk in the spirit, where he can hear from God, and be directed in how to deal with danger.

Whenever a lighthouse was set up, rules for manning the lighthouse were established. These rules seem to be somewhat universal. The keeper of the lighthouse was allowed to have some relief. Often families lived in the lighthouse, but usually two men manned it, so a lifestyle developed around the keeping of the Light. I cannot stress enough how important it is to develop this lifestyle of being alert, attentive, and sober in the Spirit.

In modern times the men stayed for one month on and three weeks off. When the guard was changed, all the supplies and provisions were taken into the storage areas first. The relief man was put aboard the lighthouse, so the house was never left unattended. After he was on and settled into his routine, the relieved man left the lighthouse. This protocol has been carried out throughout the history of lighthouses. It is extremely important that the lighthouse be manned at all times.

For a family this was a life of hardship many times. Children of keepers had to learn to sleep with the house full of bright light. The keeper had to be awake when everyone else was asleep.

Often, the family was given a parcel of land and a house connected to the lighthouse. It was dangerous for small children playing, so the parents had to keep a close eye on the little ones as well. If the father were to pass away, sometimes the wife was given his job, if she were capable of doing the job. Many keepers taught the whole family the functions of the watchman. This is a good rule to follow. Your children will always have and inheritance if you adopt the lifestyle that accompanies this ministry.

A very dangerous area of keeping is the channel off the coast of England and France, especially and the ends of the Channel. Several of the lighthouses are little more than fortresses set upon rocks.

One that is notorious for its danger is Ar-Men, a French light. In order to reach Ar-Men, the keepers have to be hoisted on by a cable connected to a boat several feet away. Because of the dangerous crags close to the rock, the boat cannot come close enough to dock. It is said that, because of bad weather and high winds it once took 21 days from start to finish to relieve the keepers and bring on more provision.

Protocol could not be broken. The keeper is never allowed to leave his watch until he is relieved, or unburdened.

LIGHTHOUSE RESCUE EFFORTS

What happened if there was a shipwreck? In the early days of lighthouse keeping, it was a painful dilemma that no keeper wanted to find himself in. Because most lighthouses were located on remote reefs, rocks, and even small islands in the middle of the ocean, the lighthouse keeper had to wait for relief to come before he could leave the house, just as we have to wait sometimes for our answers to prayer, or wait on God for revelation to take us to the next step.

Most keepers lived with family. Often a single man held that job. There were some women lighthouse keepers. Often if a woman was a keeper's widow, she was well trained for the job and as mentioned previously, could replace him as keeper. There were no hard and fast rules governing emergencies. Always the chief priority was to KEEP THE LIGHT BURNING. That light meant life, and it was far more important to save many lives than a few.

One famous case of a keeper making a rescue was that of a fifteen-year-old girl named Ann Darling. She was the daughter of the lighthouse keeper who kept a light off the coast of England. Ann woke up one morning to the sound of cries for help. She looked out of her bedroom window and saw survivors of a shipwreck sitting on a rock several miles from the lighthouse.

The storm was still raging, but she and her father took their boat and risked their own lives to rescue the eight persons who had survived the wreck. This was very unusual and risky for a keeper. They often had to watch people drown because they were unable to leave the lighthouse unattended. It was considered extremely unwise to risk their lives for the rescue.

Imagine having to listen to cries of help, and not be able to do anything because in terms of your job, your own life was more valuable than that of the ones who could not find their way to safety. As spiritual watchmen, we have more resources to help. Our job can never be abandoned, but our prayers enable us to do the job of rescue.

Also, We must never see our function as "second rate," or as a stepping-stone to a "better job." Once anointed for watching, we are watchmen for life. This is a lifetime call.

In recent times the Coast Guard in the United States, and similar rescue organizations in other nations have taken on the job of rescue, as it was risky for the lighthouse keeper to both watch and rescue. If the watchman lost his life in a rescue attempt, then more lives would be lost because the light would not be attended. In recent times, lighthouses have become automated and with electric lights that need little tending, just periodic maintenance.

The duties of watching and rescue have developed into separate specialties. In the Kingdom of God, the jobs are still combined. The watchman sees, warns, and ministers to help those who are in need.

THE KEEPER OF THE LIGHT

Much more can be said about the natural watchman. The person who keeps the light must have discipline and a sense of contentment with both the routine and ordinary functions of trimming wicks, polishing glass, changing light bulbs, and the like.

Watchmen must have a great deal of stamina, both for climbing the stairs that lead to the tower, and for solving problems that might require extra time and effort until they are resolved. The job of the light keeper is one of keen responsibility. He knows that he is the only one who can do his job. He must shoulder this responsibility with dignity and sobriety.

Many lives are dependent upon his keeping his routine watch. The watchman must learn how to keep himself mentally alert and stimulated while he entertains himself when his duties are not as pressing. Watching is a lonely job. The keeper of the light must learn how to cope with the pressures of loneliness, and gain satisfaction in knowing that many lives were saved because he stood upon his watch, and did his routine job. He is never seen and never known, but his work has preserved the lives of many. He has kept many from going shipwreck.

BEWARE OF FALSE LIGHT

It must be said here that the confidence that the mariner has in the light that comes from the lighthouse can be used against him. Pirates have been known to start huge bonfires or set up lights onshore to guide the sailor toward them. The unsuspecting sailor was then captured by these bandits. Ships have been stolen and the entire crew killed by these "false keepers."

There is little or no way for the mariner to discern true from false light from a distance. He must rely on gut instinct or feelings. Official lighthouses are those sanctioned, designed, and built by legitimate governments. They are manned by well-trained, reliable keepers, whose main aim is to guide the navigator safely to shore.

How heartless the pirate must be to take advantage of the poor, trusting sailor who depends upon the light for guidance.

The church has always been plagued with spiritual false light. Men's wisdom masquerades as revelation. The devil sends quick, easy answers to spiritual questions, which are quickly adopted by persons who trust in their own wisdom, which is another type of false light. As you can see, there develops a system of false, superficial knowledge, which produces little fruit and is void of power.

The one thing most religious leaders agree upon is that the church lacks power. The power to convert the soul, the power to deliver, the power to heal the sick and raise the dead are grossly lacking in the church, we all agree. What we don't agree upon is the method necessary to bring power back to the church. We are in desperate need of power, and if we do not discern true revelation, we will grab at the first "light" that appears.

It is extremely important that we understand all aspects of any ministry that we undertake. When I first began to pray about this ministry, I asked the Lord was who would train me for this ministry. I am shocked that in the information age we assume so much knowledge, especially the knowledge of God. We often feel that if we cannot get it in the local church, that we do not need it. How sad to put the knowledge of God on such a superficial and shallow level. This is one reason that the church lacks power: too much assumption, and too little study and preparation.

I think of all the great leaders of the church who have devoted their lives to the study of God's Word and demonstrating the power of the Holy Spirit, and I wonder if the average church going believer understands the amount of time spent in study, prayer and developing relationship with God that it takes to have power in one's hands to heal the sick. The question for us in the church is, "will we continue to measure our success by mere numbers, or will we judge by fruit?" How do we produce the fruit of God?

The answer is found in Ephesians 4:11. Until the church grows into maturity and quits being afraid to go to conferences, Bible studies, schools of ministry and learn how to minister under the anointing, we will never attain the fullness of the stature of Christ. The ministry of the watchman is an important part of this maturing process. This ministry teaches believers to do the works of God.

"The gross darkness that is now sweeping the earth will increase and increase until the body of Christ has had enough of trying to blend in and hide herself.

"She will emerge from her sleep as Samson did, shake herself of her compromise and pant after her Lord. She will be driven to follow hard after me," says the Lord, "she will follow hard after me.

"She will submit to sound doctrine and I will anoint her with miracle working power afresh and anew. I will anoint her as she awakens to her true purpose and true identity," *says the Lord of Hosts."*

Given through Barbara A. Williams, May 2, 2000

"The best of them is as a brier: the most upright is sharper than a thorn hedge: the day of thy watchmen and thy visitation cometh; now shall be their perplexity. Trust ye not in a friend, put ye not confidence in a guide: keep the doors of thy mouth from her that lieth in thy bosom." Micah 7:4-5

CHAPTER SIX

Natural Watchmen are Similar to Spiritual Watchmen

"But ye shall receive power, after that the Holy Ghost is come upon you: and ye shall be witnesses unto me both in Jerusalem, and in all Judea, and in Samaria, and unto the uttermost part of the earth." Acts 1:8

We can learn a great deal through observing natural things. For instance, Jesus taught in parables. The Bible says that God may speak *first one way and then another, yet man does not perceive it. (Job 33:15).* Observing natural watchman will give us insight into the structure of the ministry of the spiritual watchman.

The role of watchman as defender of the faith can be seen as we observe the armed forces and law enforcement personnel who guard our country. Just as the natural protection agencies have specific territories and duties, so our spiritual "armed forces" have outlined duties and areas of activity.

The prophet and those in his company defends the faith by confronting spiritual governments. Through intercession, he is able to ward off the attacking spirits and therefore enforce what "is written." When Jesus said, "it is written," He was telling Satan that there was a law in effect that had already sealed his doom. This is what the watchman must be keenly aware of. If we understand that God has already spoken on all issues, that the scriptures are sealed and cannot be broken, amended or added to, then we can be assured when we enforce God's laws that He backs us up.

THE LOCAL POLICEMAN:
PRAYING FOR YOUR JERUSALEM

Everyone is familiar with the role and function of the local police officer. The watchman functions in a very similar way.

He has a "set" watch that he must keep, similar to that of a "beat" for a policeman. God has defined your "beat" in His Word. Our first watch is always over our families. We guard their souls and pray until everyone in our households are saved. We call it "household salvation."

"And if it seem evil unto you to serve the Lord, choose you this day whom ye will serve; whether the gods which your fathers served that were on the other side of the flood, or the gods of the Amorites, in whose land ye dwell: but as for me and my house, we will serve the Lord." Joshua 24:15

We understand from Joshua 24:15 that God has called our houses to be saved and serve the Lord. We guard over this and begin to rebuke the devil if he appears to be working to deceive our loved ones.

We bind rebellion in our children, and pray for them to choose the right companions because we are enforcing a law that is already written:

"And all thy children shall be taught of the Lord; and great shall be the peace of thy children." Isaiah 54:13

When we begin this or any prayer ministry, there are rules that govern our scope of responsibility and authority. Very simply, the anointing that you possess determines the scope of your authority, while your relationships and lifestyle determine your responsibility.

Your authority will also depend upon your level of knowledge, revelation, and relationship of submission to ministry gifts that exercise authority by virtue of their anointing. In other words, you will receive what you study. You will have imparted to you what your teachers possess.

We all know that two persons can pray the same prayer, and one will get results and the other will not. Whether or not one gets results depends upon whether or not God honors that prayer. The prayer that is anointed will be honored and get the results. The prayer must be prayed in faith.

Faith determines the anointing. We've all been in meetings where people shouted real loud, clapped and stomped and the devil never moved. Even though the *presence* of God is in their midst, the ***anointing*** of God was not there to do the job. There is a difference between the presence and the anointing. They may be believers, but they are not anointed for that specific task.

The worst thing one can do is assume an anointing that he does not possess, or to try to "claim" an anointing. The anointing is not "claimed," it is conferred by God. It flows with the level of knowledge a person has of The Word and is in line with and specific to the gift of God that person possesses and the work to which he is called.

Anointings are specific. We know this from Old Testament study. There were three anointings available to Old Testament saints: that of prophet, king, or priest. They were not interchangeable and did not overlap. Some men and women walked in the fullness of their offices, others carried out their duties in a very shallow way. Some got in trouble for trying to carry out the duties of an office to which they were not called.

When King Saul attempted to function in the priests' and prophet's offices, (1 Samuel 15) he was removed from the office of King. God still holds the specifics of the anointing he gives to us in high esteem.

Learn how the anointing operates, and learn how to function in the one that you are called to possess. Not all believers have the same anointing, just as we all can't wear the same size clothes.

THE COUNTY OR STATE TROOPER:
PRAYING FOR YOUR JUDEA

The next level of watching involves taking on a greater level of anointing and responsibility. This function works in your neighborhood, workplace, or local geographical area. God must promote you to a higher level as you begin to become burdened to see change in the souls around you.

Now don't get me wrong, we all want people to treat us better, be kinder to us, and so on, but the change I am speaking of is the type that leads to more godliness. We are concerned that these individuals lead a better life. We often may offer prayer if problems arise, or we may speak to them more freely about God, and salvation, and determine whether they are saved. These people become our focus outside of our normal family watch.

I guess we could liken this role to that of a County Sheriff or a State trooper. After the family is secured, then God gives us the authority and the anointing to affect broader areas. He gives this to us because of our demonstrated faithfulness over our house.

God only promotes faithful people. If we cannot have faith for our loved ones, how can we have faith for a whole nation or even our cities? When God sees that we believe that we have received that which we pray for, he promotes us, even if all the things we pray for have not yet come to pass.

I frequently warn people about being concerned for China and neglecting the needs of their loved ones. Often we are caught up in the church system. We hear testimonies of great things others are doing for God, and we seek to out-do that person. There is a great lack of love in this type of motivation, and God cannot use us if our motives are not pure.

The greatest act of Godliness and humility may not come from the person who wins an important person to the Lord, but it may come to the wife who continues to endure embarrassment because of an alcoholic or drug addicted husband. The reward comes when this person wakes up in his right mind free from the torment of drug demons.

All of our relatives are persons for whom Christ shed His blood. We need to honor them and hold them in high esteem. The love of God shows no partiality. We should love our family members as ourselves.

When God moves us to this next level of watching, He will begin to open new doors of utterance for us. When God opens the door for you to minister to someone, there is peace. I have seen many people try to force themselves into positions of ministry. This is never God. He cannot anoint rebellious and angry flesh. You may see great needs, but God knows when the time is right for the utterance that you speak.

Trust Him. When doors open, you may notice that people with problems will come to you for help. Be careful not to give advice, but pray and ask God to fill your mouth with words. He may lead you to invite these people to your local church or to a teaching or healing meeting. Know that you are their link to God and His power. Be faithful with what He gives you.

THE FEDERAL AGENT:
PRAYING FOR YOUR NATION

Anyone who feels burdened when watching the news or reading the paper knows this level of watching. When I speak of watching, I mean an area that God speaks to you personally to pray for. Many times we are assigned prayers when we are a part of a group, but if we carry a specific anointing, we will be called upon to use that anointing to see to it that a particular mission is carried out to the end.

Prayer watches are not something you become involved in for a brief time, but you are called to a watch to carry it out until the fulfillment of God's will.

Think of the people who prayed for years against communism. First the Berlin Wall, then the Soviet Union. I am sure that there were many watchmen in those countries who were not allowed to quit. Some went home to be with the Lord before they saw the fulfillment of the promise, but others were present when the walls fell.

This level of prayer will affect the political climate in which we live, because the anointing that comes with this type of prayer is aimed at the seats of governments. All governments are natural governments that have demonic princes in control over them. Since Satan is the god of this world, he has set a hierarchy and system of demonic spirits in power over the earth.

"For we wrestle not against flesh and blood, but against principalities, against powers, against the rulers of the darkness of this world, against spiritual wickedness in high places." Ephesians 6:12

"Which he wrought in Christ, when he raised him from the dead, and set him at his own right hand in the heavenly places, Far above all principality, and power, and might, and dominion, and every name that is named, not only in this world, but also in that which is to come:" Ephesians 1:20-21

These entities, and not people, are always the focus of the prayers of the watchman. There will be times when we preach the good news to people. We may even warn (Ezek. 3:8) those who are out of the way. We always pray for the needs of people, but in order to get at the root of the problem, we must address the spirit controlling the situation. Without thorough study of the Bible and a system of prayer that contains this revelation, we may find that our prayers are frustrated and hindered, because they do not quite hit the mark.

This is why the study of warfare is essential to the watchman. I can think of no government that functions without a protective body called out of its body of citizens. These agents must be adequately trained, often by many years of study, discipline, and hard work. There is such a force in the body of Christ. We are a quiet but effective group of servants. We are watchmen.

THE CIA: THE INTERNATIONAL WATCHMAN
STUDYING THE STRATEGIES OF THE ENEMY

God may choose to use you to travel to foreign nations. I am not speaking here of the trips many Christians take where they see some famous preacher on TV, pay their money and go on a once in a lifetime trip to see what that minister does with the money you send. I am not talking about Christian cruises where singers and musician entertain the guests. I'm talking about being a "sent one" in the apostolic and prophetic sense. You can be sent for a brief period of time, a season, or you may be sent again and again. Apostles and prophets are sent because of the anointing and ability that they have to dislodge and bind principalities. They are sent by command, not necessarily invitation. They often choose people who work with them on a regular basis to accompany them, and go into that country and pray for a door to be opened for the preaching of the gospel.

This was true in the case of Charles Finney and Brother Nash. Brother Nash traveled ahead of Brother Finney, and as a watchman set a watch and battled the Prince of the city just before Finney arrived. Brother Nash spent time observing the spiritual activities of the city when he arrived.

Many times God will begin to speak to the watchman about the plans of the enemy, and then give a strategy of prayer to bind the enemy's power and stop the enemy's advance before the preaching begins. When Finney called the meeting, hundreds and thousands showed up.

Brother Nash was a prophet sent ahead of the Apostle Finney. He was a watchman because he stayed set until the atmosphere was right for the preaching of the gospel by Charles Finney.

The watchman sees the world as one place, and not a group of nations with barriers when God calls him to this level of warfare. The more you grow in God the smaller the world becomes. Prophets and Apostles must be anointed at this level of watching in order to affect the world for the gospel.

This is obedience to the great commission to go into all the world and preach the gospel to every creature. Before one can be sent to preach certain truths, the way must be made through prayer that binds evil princes. This is a function of the watchman.

THE APOSTLE-PROPHET AS WATCHMAN

We have just mentioned that some ministers will send prayer teams into a city before they go in to do their actual ministry. This also can be done sovereignly by God through the use of the watchman, especially the watchman who functions in the ministry gift offices of the Apostle and/or Prophet. The more the watchman can function strictly by the spirit, the more effective he is.

Dr. Lester Sumrall was perhaps the most accomplished in this ministry that we know of today. Dr. Sumrall talks of his work in the Philippines, which began when he prayed all night for a young woman who was being tormented by demons. While watching the evening news, Dr. Sumrall was disturbed at the account of a sixteen-year-old girl, a convicted street prostitute who was imprisoned. She had placed a curse on a jailer who later died. She also was being tormented and bitten by the demons that possessed her.

After *praying for her in his home,* Brother Sumrall felt the Lord leading him to visit her in order *to minister to her.* In this case, his prayers both opened the door for ministry and empowered him to do the ministry. With great compassion, Brother Sumrall ministered to the young woman, led her to the Lord, and after a few years of walking with God, this young lady was married with a family.

Brother Sumrall says he believes he confronted the strongman of that city, a spirit of witchcraft and false religion that had not only this young girl, but also the whole town captive and bound in fear. His anointing carried him to international territory. He went by faith. When he first began, no church supported him, and no devil stopped him.

He went by command of the Lord, the anointing that he possessed being the only currency that he used.

 *"Go your ways: behold, I send you forth as lambs among wolves. Carry neither purse, nor scrip, nor shoes: and salute no man by the way." Luke 10:3-4*

The anointing will open any door that needs to be opened, and subdue any kingdom that opposes you. When you are anointed to do these types of exploits for God, you don't need man to affirm you, or to open doors for you or send invitations to you. You need only obey the unction of the Spirit.

A NOTE ABOUT THE CORPORATE ANOINTING

When we pray in a group led by a prophet, there is an anointing in the atmosphere that is carried by the leader. This anointing is for his ministry and upon his ministry.

That is why it is easy to pray in this type of setting and may be more difficult for the student to pray at home or in another atmosphere. Many persons will assume that because they pray with ease in a corporate setting that they possess or carry that same anointing as an individual that the leader possesses. This is not true.

While it is possible to possess that anointing, it may not have been conferred upon the individual as of yet. As a disciple of the senior prophet, the student must stay in the place of learning until the full price is paid and God places the anointing that you have paid for upon you permanently.

"Watch and pray, that ye enter not into temptation: the spirit indeed is willing, but the flesh is weak." Matthew 26:41

CHAPTER SEVEN

Positions of the Watchman: Sit, Stand, and Walk

SIT: RULERSHIP AND AUTHORITY

And what is the exceeding greatness of his power to us-ward who believe, according to the working of his mighty power, which he wrought in Christ, when he raised him from the dead, and set him at his own right hand in the heavenly places...

Even when we were dead in sins, hath quickened us together with Christ, (by grace ye are saved;)

And hath raised us up together, and made us sit together in heavenly places in Christ Jesus.
Ephesians 1:19-20; 2:5-6.

Notice that the watchman has a post in which he **sits.** This is his seat of authority. It is from this position that he occupies and can guard the area to which he is assigned.

The watchman makes routine rounds of all the "portals of entry" to prevent the enemy from stealing or disturbing what he is guarding. There is certain real property that is entrusted to the watchman.

He may watch over houses, lands, jobs, relationships, and property. He must guard these things with all diligence. His most important watch, however, is over the souls of men.

The watchman functions uniquely in the position of rulership on behalf of the Lord. The scriptures clearly state that Jesus has given us the keys to the kingdom of God. These keys open the kingdom to the earth or shut it up from manifesting down here on earth.

 *And I will give unto thee the keys of the kingdom of heaven: and whatsoever thou shalt bind on earth shall be bound in heaven: and whatsoever thou shalt loose on earth shall be loosed in heaven.*
Matthew 16:19

Whatever we allow on earth is allowed by heaven; whatever we disallow on earth is disallowed by heaven. This power of the watchman is similar to that of a typical night watchman.

The night watchman has a station from which he can observe the area he has been given to protect. He knows how to protect this area by his training.

If his area is large, he may make frequent rounds to check areas where the enemy may hide, or where someone may break in and steal. This is what we do; we keep the devil from stealing. The watchman knows what activities are suspicious by his discernment and knowledge of patterns of the thief's behavior. The watchman must have perfect confidence in his authority to seek out, apprehend and stop or arrest any intruder.

By doing this, the watchman is able to secure an area so that the rightful owners can carry out their normal duties in peace. This is the end result of all spiritual warfare: peace.

STAND: OCCUPYING UNTIL HE COMES

And having done all (your watch), to stand. Stand therefore, having your loins girt about with truth, and having on the breastplate of righteousness;

And your feet shod with the preparation of the gospel of peace; Above all, taking the shield of faith, wherewith ye shall be able to quench all the fiery darts of the wicked.

And take the helmet of salvation, and the sword of the Spirit, which is the word of God: Praying always with all prayer and supplication in the Spirit, and watching thereunto with all perseverance and supplication for all saints. Ephesians 6:13-18

After the watchman has made his rounds, inspected and secured his territory, then he stands guard over what God has entrusted to him. He has entrusted His promises to all of us. Every promise of blessing written in the book of the law is ours. God expects us to receive these promises as an inheritance.

We are promised personal blessings, and blessings related to our position of service in the kingdom. For instance, God has promised us *household salvation.* This is a very simple promise to see from the scriptures.

From the garden, we see promises to the man and woman, *and their seed.* When Noah was saved, he was saved, *and his house.* The last example that comes to my mind is Cornelius in Acts chapter 10. This man was a Roman centurion who obtained favor with God, and his whole house was saved in one day.

Well, guess what? The devil will fight you concerning this very scripture. A common strategy I see him using today to discourage us from praying and standing in faith for household salvation is divorce. Many times people will make a stand and pray until the spouse divorces them.

Sometimes a Christian may turn angry and bitter and divorce the unsaved loved one after years of praying for their salvation. Well, did God mean what He said when He promised to save everybody in your house? Did He not know that the divorce was coming, and He made the promise anyway? So why would you change your position?

There is enough faith in God to bring even the most impossible things to pass. Resume your stand on God's

Word. Make the devil a liar. Continue to stand for the soul of your spouse even after divorce. We have a ministry of reconciliation to a God who commands us to love, not hate. God never changes His promises, no matter what man does. They are still called to be saved by your prayers.

WALK: FELLOWSHIP WITH GOD
THE MIND OF CHRIST

 ***This I say then, Walk in the Spirit, and ye shall not fulfill the lust of the flesh. Galatians 5:16***

We have the mind of Christ. 2 Corinthians 2:16

The watchman is called to walk with God in His realm every day. Walking with God is not something that you can get from an instruction book, but it is a way of life that comes through relationship, surrender, and obedience to God.

Walking with God means walking in faith. We must trust God and obey His word. We must study His word to know what His thoughts are, and then meditate on His word day and night. This is something that takes practice, but is well worth it when we see the fruit.

Many times we want to launch out into the deep and do mighty things for God, when we rebel at obeying Him in the small things. We must remember to obey God *in all things*. When we have this spirit of surrender, then God finds the fellowship with us sweet and he begins to share more and more with us.

We must walk in love to be in harmony with God. A complaining, bitter, discouraged, or anguished spirit causes Him to withdraw from us. If we could only discipline ourselves to draw nearer to Him when our thoughts keep us down!

We have been duped by the devil to think that it is "normal" to feel depressed or discouraged. These feelings are normal for the carnal man, or the sinner, but not for the born-again spirit man. Sometimes we must fight to stay in there, but we can overcome the problems that attack our minds, because Jesus has already overcome them for us.

I believe we can grow out of our problems if we cannot have them all resolved. Growing in the fruit of the spirit, keeping ourselves in joy and in love is the only remedy for problems. Problems are what you make of them. I decided to drop certain words from my vocabulary. Problem was one of them.

I don't live in denial, I LIVE IN FAITH and in the realm of answers. Why should I dwell on the wrong, when God has given the right through His word? I immediately search for an answer in God's Word when a problem comes up. I do this on purpose.

It is a discipline. Daily renewing our minds in The Word of God will keep us on course. It is surprising what a twenty-minute refreshing in The Word will do for us. In order to be effective, we must walk in the spirit of love.

Forgiveness and letting go are essential to keeping harmony with God. We are commanded to walk in the fruit of the spirit and avoid the lusts of the flesh. How often do we forgive a person, or say we do, and yet our thoughts about that person are continually negative.

We dwell on the harm they have done us, or the fact that they have disappointed us. Each time we dwell here, we push God further away. Many people park here, as though they're enjoying a wonderful sunset. This reverie regarding past hurts and disappointments is a grief to God, since Jesus has paid for them to be removed.

Often it is an act of pride when we continue to dwell on these past offenses. We are determined to have our own way. Often we feel that we *can't stop* thinking about certain past hurts, but we can. Reverie in God's word will do it. Witness or pray for someone. This will cause the negative thought pattern to be broken. Bless that person who cursed you, when possible.

These are the activities of an over comer. God wants us to focus on our wonderful present and glorious future with Him, not some petty offense that is dead and buried with Christ. Overcomers rise up in resurrection power. When you walk continually in the power that raised Christ Jesus from the dead, you walk as He walks now on the earth. You are regularly seated in heavenly places with Him. He gives you strategies that cause you to triumph over all obstacles. You have the ability to stand where He has placed you and occupy until the manifestation comes.

The following prophecy was given to me to encourage all believers who would dare take a stand for the Lord. I pray that it will encourage you to stand in faith and be valiant in battle:

Subduing the Enemy Under Your Feet

Prophecy given through Barbara A. Williams
August 14, 1999

The Lord wants you to know that the enemy that is the strongest against you, He will subdue under your feet. The enemy

that is the strongest against you; the one that you thought you'd never see the end of this battle. You would never see the end of this accusation against you. You would never see the end of this plot against you; this device and this wickedness against you. The Lord wants you to know that that is the young lion--the lion of strength that has been sent against your life to destroy it, to pull it down, to cause it not to be what the Lord has called it to be.

"But I," says the Lord, "am the one that has put the young lion in your face that you may confront him so that I might show Myself strong on your behalf," says the Lord. "For you will subdue every enemy under your feet," says the Spirit of God. "You will confront every foe that would try to raise and rear its ugly head against you," saith the Lord. "And you will do it such a way that I will get honor on this enemy," says the Spirit of God. "For I will subdue every enemy under My feet," says the Lord. "And I have plans and I have purposes for your life, and I have to show every wicked foe that comes against you that I am God," saith the Lord.

"For I have more business to do in your life than you could ever imagine. I have much kingdom business to do in your life," says the Lord. "And I have much to prove to the enemy who accuses the brethren day and night," says the Spirit of God. "I have much to prove to the devil that would accuse Me about you day and night," says the Spirit of God. "For I have much to show him about your character, and I have much to show him about your commitment, and I have

much to show him about your dedication to me," says the Spirit of God. "And when all enemies are subdued under your feet," says the Spirit of God, "then you will trample on all of them," says the Spirit of the Lord. "You will skip over them as though they are nothing," says the Spirit of God.

"So I want you to stay firm and stay tight in what I have given you," says the Spirit. "Stay firm and stay right in My anointing. Stay firm and stay right in My truth," says the Spirit of God. "Stay firm and stay right with me. Dwell under the shadow of the Almighty. Cry out to Me when it is too much for you. Strengthen yourself in Me when you need to be strengthened," says the Lord, "for I am there for you. I am your help and I am your stay! You don't have to try and do this on your own," says the Spirit of God. "But come to Me when you need to talk to me, and I can share strategy with you and I can share My heart and My mind with you," says the Spirit of God.

"And I will not stop," says the Lord. "I will not stop. I WILL NOT STOP UNTIL EVERY ENEMY IS YOUR FOOTSTOOL! " says the Spirit of the Living God.

"Set up the standard upon the walls of Babylon, make the watch strong, set up the watchmen, prepare the ambushes: for the Lord hath both devised and done that which he spake against the inhabitants of Babylon." Jeremiah 51:12

"Blessed are those servants, whom the Lord when He cometh shall find watching..." Luke 12:37a

CHAPTER EIGHT

The Best is Yet to Come!

As we look forward to the day when the Lord returns, I see a glorious future ahead for the Church. God has given so much to us as believers. We have so many weapons of warfare. We have a degree of revelation that is unmatched by any generation in the history of the church.

The knowledge that has been released about faith, the Holy Spirit, and the ministry gifts and the believer's ministry is very valuable. We should never take these things for granted, but we should be very diligent in our pursuit of the knowledge of God.

With so much knowledge of the correct way to pray, to acquire faith, and so much mobility among believers to travel to extra meetings and conferences, even to attend ongoing schools of ministry like the one we have here at the Ministry of the Watchman, it will be very difficult for any believer who is not knowledgeable in the correct way to minister to have any excuse when he stands before the Lord.

With knowledge and responsibility comes accountability. We will answer to the Lord when He asks us why we did not attend certain meetings to obtain certain knowledge or impartation when the meeting was held right in our own town, or was a short drive away.

Often we think that we are waiting for God to show us someone who needs to be ministered to. Actually Jesus said these words,

Say not ye, There are yet four months, and then cometh harvest? Behold, I say unto you, Lift up your eyes, and look on the fields; for they are white already to harvest. John 4:35

This means that anybody who sees as Jesus sees knows that there are always people who need the Lord. We need to equip ourselves as laborers, and know that there is the work of harvest available to us at all times. The following prophecies explain what God desires to do in us in order to fully equip us for the harvest.

CR   SO

Develop a Prophetic Ear

*An excerpt from the Prophecy
given through Barbara Williams, March 18, 2000*

"For there is coming a sound," says the Spirit of God. "There is coming a sound into the earth," says the Lord. "There is coming a sound," says the Spirit, "that not everybody will be able to hear; not everybody who calls themselves by My name will be able to hear," says the Lord. "There is a sound coming into the earth," says the Spirit.

"And it is a sound of many waters. It is a sound of hoof beats. It is a sound of a rushing mighty wind. It is a sound of urgency," says the Spirit. "It is a sound of intensity," says the Spirit of God.

"It is a sound," says the Lord, "that will bring the miraculous, will bring the dramatic, will bring the instantaneous into the earth in a great, great measure," says the Spirit of God. "And already that sound is manifesting— a little bit here and a little bit there. And some people don't

recognize the sound; others—they recognize it," says the Lord.

"So cultivate a listening ear," says the Spirit of God. "Cultivate a listening ear," says the Spirit. "Cultivate a listening ear," says the Spirit. "For the things of <u>MY SPIRIT</u>," says the Spirit of God. "For the things that pertain to Me," says the Spirit of God. "For many will run here and there LOOKING," says the Lord, "but it will not be a matter of SEEING but it will be a matter of HEARING," says the Spirit. "It will be a matter of hearing accurately," says the Lord. "And understanding what you hear, and interpreting what you hear accurately by My Spirit," says the Lord. "So the only way that one can hear it," says the Spirit of God, "is to develop a prophetic ear. Develop a listening ear to the things of the Spirit that I announce, the things of the Spirit that I give sound to, the things of the Spirit that I give voice to," says the Lord. "For there are many sounds in the earth," says the Spirit of God, "and none of them are without significance," says the Lord.

"But the coming move will be a move where people will have to know the sounds," says the Spirit. "There are sounds that I have yet to release into the earth," says the Lord. "There are sounds that I must declare. There's a tuning in and a fine-tuning into the hearing of My people that I must do," says the Spirit, "so that they can hear and accurately move in and accurately receive what I have, that they might use it, that they might bless people, that they might serve humanity with the things that I send.

"And so the sound of the hoof beat, the sound of the roaring, the sound of the intensity, the sound of something that is stirring," says the Spirit. "The sound of a rotor," says the Spirit of God. "That whirring sound—the sound of the whirlwind," says the Spirit of God, "is coming into the earth. And those who catch that sound, and follow that sound, and obey that sound will be equipped," says the Lord. "Those who hear that sound and follow that sound and catch that sound will be fulfilled. They will be made ready. They will be empowered. They will have the things that they need. There will be a sound to call them to run to safety, and there will be a sound to call them to advance. There will be a sound to call them to press in and there will be a sound to call them to gather in," says the Spirit...

Cultivating The Fruit of Love in God's Army

An excerpt from the Prophecy given through Barbara A. Williams, March 4, 2000

"Abide in My love," says the Lord. "Abide in My love," says the Spirit of God. "For the season is yet to come," says the Spirit, "where I can trust all of My body," says the Spirit of God. "All of My body," says the Lord. "Because love is something that has escaped most of humanity in this hour," says the Spirit.

"For the enemy has assaulted and assaulted and assaulted the earth with hatred and violence and malice and rebellion and witchcraft," says the Spirit of God.

"And I need those who can walk in love. I need those who can forgive because love never fails," says the Spirit. "Love is the power that overcomes," says the Lord. "For the faith must be there," says the Spirit, "for that is the overcoming power. But faith only works by love," says the Lord. "So love is the greatest," says the Spirit.

"For it is time for another fruit to be poured out on My people in the earth," says the Lord. "For I am the one who adorns the priesthood. I am the one who fits the priest with his robe and the robe is adorned and finished off by a bell and a pomegranate and a bell and a pomegranate and a bell and a pomegranate," says the Spirit of God. "The pomegranate of course represents the fruit. The bell represents the gift of the Holy Ghost. The gift of prophecy, the gift of the discerning of spirits, the gift of the unction that functions within you to lead you and guide you into all truth," says the Lord.

"And so the gift must always be tempered with the fruit," says the Spirit. "For the fruit of Love must flow in My body," says the Lord. "The fruit of love that brings joy and brings laughter. The fruit of love that brings great forgiveness. The fruit of love that allows the person to go the extra mile," says the Spirit. "The fruit of love that causes one never to give up," says the Spirit of God.

"For many times we look at those who can accomplish much in My body," says the Spirit. "We look at those of great accomplishment," says the Lord.

"And we look at those people and we try to figure out," says the Lord, *"what it is that causes them to have this great success. And at the end of everything,"* says the Spirit of God, *"it is their great love for Me, their great love for humanity, their ability to forgive, their ability to believe the best, their ability to continue to hold on when everybody else has given up and everybody else has said, 'it will not work and it will fail',"* says the Spirit.

"It is love that causes one to endure," says the Spirit of God. *"It is love that causes one not to give up,"* says the Spirit, *"because love has the ability to tell the person that it is still possible. Love has the ability to tell the person that they can still do it. Love has the ability to tell the person that they can accomplish much in Me,"* says the Spirit of God.

"And so when My body and My bride are seated with Me in heavenly places, it is because of their great love for Me and their great love for humanity that allows them to be seated next to Me," says the Spirit of God. *"It is that quality in them that causes them to be elevated above the ways of the world and above the dictates of the flesh and above the dictates of the carnal mind,"* says the Spirit of God. *"It is their great love,"* says the Spirit, *"that allows that person to ascend to the highest heights and know that they can ride upon the high places,"* says the Spirit of God, *"because love never fails—it has that ability to tell that person that they can do all things through Me who strengthens them because of their great love,"* says the Spirit of God ...

ɞ ଣ

Obedience to Move to the Next Level

An excerpt from the Prophecy given through Barbara Williams
March 25, 2000

"The time of high obedience," says the Lord. "The time of high obedience is upon the earth," says the Spirit of God. "The time of high obedience is upon the earth," says the Spirit of the Living God. "This is the time," says the Lord, "to obey Me and only Me. You must close out all other voices. You must close out reasonings. You must cast down imaginations. You must cast down arguments. You can no longer afford to argue with the wisdom behind My words," says the Spirit of God. "You can no longer afford to wrestle with emotional things," says the Lord.

"You can no longer afford to walk in insecurity," says the Spirit of God, "and not being secure in that I've called you and be willing to leave the familiar and to leave the comfortable and do as I told Abraham to do; and that is get up and go and move into a land that was not familiar to him, into a land that was not comfortable for him, into a place where he would have to move again and again," says the Spirit of God.

"Into the journey that is before you," says the Lord. "For I have placed many things before you," says the Spirit of God. "I have placed many things in your heart," says the Lord. "I have placed many visions before you," says the Spirit, "and you must have the willingness to go," says the Lord.

"You must have the willingness to obey. You must have the willingness to leave your mental domain and leave what is familiar to you in your own thinking and move out into a new realm of the renewed soul in Me," says the Spirit of the Living God. "For I have many things yet to show you," says the Lord. "I have many things that I want to do in you, I have many things I want to plant in you and to see cultivated and to see grow and to see prosper...

ℭ ℬ

Gaining Strength in Resistance

An excerpt from the Prophecy given through Barbara A. Williams, March 6, 1999

The Spirit of God wants to just exhort you and encourage you, but He does have a question: The Spirit of God would ask you, "What is opposing you? What is standing against you? What is standing in your way? What is standing between you and the promise that I have made to you? What is opposing you?" says the Lord. "What is standing against you?" says the Spirit of God. "What is that resistance?" says the Lord. "What is that mountain? What is that thing that stands against you?" says the Spirit of God.

"Is it your doubt? Is it your fear? Is it your inability to understand that in Me all things are possible; that nothing is impossible with Me? Is it your desire to do things without Me? Or your inability to know My voice and know when I'm speaking to you?" says the Lord. "What is that thing that stands between you and your victory? What is that thing

that opposes you every time you think about having your victory? What is that thing that comes against you and makes you not victorious? What is it that opposes you?" says the Spirit of God. "What is it that opposes you?" says the Spirit.

"Do you not know that My Word and My Unction are like a battering ram, " says the Spirit. "Whatever it is that My Word meets, if it resists My Word, " says the Lord, "if you would not faint, if you would back up, if you would mount up with wings as eagles, if you would wait for Me for the new word and the new unction and make up your mind that you're going to hit it again, " says the Spirit of God. "And hit it again, " says the Spirit of God. "And hit it again," says the Spirit of God. "And hit it again, and hit it again, and hit it again, and hit it again, and hit it again, do you not know, " says the Spirit of God, "that every time you are resisted, and every time you are repelled that you gain strength in Me? " says the Spirit of God...

ೞ   ಐ

God's Irresistible Love in Your Heart

An excerpt from the Prophecy given through Barbara Williams,
December 19, 1999

"Oh, the Love," says the Spirit of God. "Oh the Love of God that is shed abroad in your hearts by the Holy Ghost," says the Spirit. "Oh that I might find a vessel," says the Lord. "Oh that I might find a man or a woman," says the Spirit of God.

"Oh that I might find a vessel through whom I can spread the love of God abroad! ABROAD! ABROAD! ABROAD! ABROAD," says the Spirit of God. "That I might shed it ABROAD!" says the Spirit of God. "That I might shed in places that you may never go," says the Spirit of God.

"That I might shed it in places that you may never think to shed it," says the Spirit of God. "That it might be sent out," says the Spirit. "That I might sent out at My bidding; that it might be sent out at My beckoning; that it might be sent out at My command," says the Spirit of God. "To places that you know not," says the Spirit. "And places that you think not," says the Spirit. "And places that you don't understand it needs to go," says the Spirit of God. "That I might have a vessel that is so yielded to Me that I might shed My love ABROAD! ABROAD! ABROAD!" says the Spirit of God.

"For My love is big enough to go into those hard-to-reach places," says the Spirit. "My love is big enough to penetrate those people who are impenetrable in your eyes," says the Spirit. "My love IS powerful enough to overcome even your weakness," says the Spirit. "My love is strong enough to do every thing that I want it to do in you and through you and for everyone that you touch and those you can't even see," says the Spirit. "OH! That I might have a vessel that I can say is yielded to Me and that would obey Me and would do what I tell them to do at the appropriate TIME," says the Spirit of God.

"That your LOVE (that love that you keep to yourself. That love that you're afraid of," says the Spirit. "That love that if you would show it to somebody you think they would take advantage of you again," says the Spirit.) "YES! THAT LOVE," says the Lord. "THAT LOVE! That love that so wants to come out," says the Spirit.

"That love that so wants to be expressed," says the Spirit. "That love that you keep bottled up inside of you," says the Spirit of God. "That you think is something that CANNOT be shed out," says the Lord. "You think it's something fragile," says the Spirit of God.

"But it is powerful and it is mighty and it is strong," says the Spirit of God. "It is mightier than the voice of many waters," says the Spirit of God. "It is mighty to the pulling down of strongholds," says the Spirit of God. "It is a mighty weapon of warfare down here on earth," says the Spirit of God.

"Think not your love as being weak," says the Lord. "Don't try to hide it! Don't try to keep it from people! Don't treat it as something fragile and something weak. For it <u>does</u> want to burst forth," says the Spirit of God. "It <u>does</u> want to be shed out," says the Spirit of God.

"It is longing to touch people," says the Spirit of God. "Because it is of Me," says the Spirit. "It is living substance! It is life! It is bread! And is health to those that you might shed it to," says the Spirit of God.

Cຈ ຂD

All these prophecies, as well as other prophecies given through Rev. Williams, are available in their entirety on the prophecies page on our website: www.ministryofthewatchman.com, or you may call us at 1-800-560-9240 for a printed copy.

One Final Word

As we enter the new millennium, I reflect on the progress of this ministry from the initial vision cast over 15 years ago and am refreshed in my spirit and encouraged in my heart that God would recast the vision and strengthen our resolve to forge ahead without fear.

September 11, 2001 has placed us as believers, and especially as watchmen into positions of global significance. We know that we are able because of Him who is able to prevent us from falling and present us faultless before His throne with exceeding joy. To the Only Wise God and Father be majesty, praise, dominion and power! Amen!

~ Barbara Williams ~

~ The Unique Work ~
The Ministry of the Watchman

Prophecy given through Miriam Hellman, January 26, 2002

"I believe that this is good ground. I believe that the watchmen have (as the Lord was speaking to me), a far more profound calling than you have ever imagined. Something to do that no one else has done.

"A work that is fashioned in eternity, and waiting for the one who will wear its equipping as a permanent garment. (That is what the Lord is saying to you [Barbara]) It's waiting to be worn as a permanent garment. Not a work that is similar. Not a work that is committed to a few, but a single work, only committed to you – UNIQUE.

A UNIQUENESS... The Lord wants to fashion this ministry in a uniqueness beyond its wildest dream. Unique and precise for the hour.

And the Lord says He will make you UNTOUCHABLE.

Though many will not understand, and will insist that you shouldn't go that way, yet you will go. And the Lord says, 'because way, way, way back in the beginning of the call – before you became involved in the call – that's what you really wanted.' And He's going to give it! And all the involvement in the call is important because the ministry and the people are in place. But now your place – your placement in Him – is rising.

And it may leave some behind because they cannot comprehend it, but you are forging your position in eternity. And the Lord says, 'Remember eternity. Never worry about the moment because greatness awaits you.'

And you're at a threshold. And you're at a stairway in the Spirit. And every step, the step gets smaller. It starts with a wide base, and then it narrows and narrows, and becomes more constricted as you reach the higher ground. But because you walk it, and you achieve it, you will bring many to this place. Because the Lord is not coming only for people who are being delivered from the fires of hell; He is coming for a bride that is perfected in every way. And he is asking you to turn your attention to the perfection of highly skilled workmen in His Kingdom. And you'll work a work that only has the name of 'THE MINISTRY OF THE WATCHMAN' over it. And no others can do it – only you."

BIBLIOGRAPHY

Chase, Mary Ellen, **The Story of Lighthouses,** 1965, W.W. Norton, New York, NY

Gleason, Sarah C., <u>Kindly Lights,</u> 1991 Beacon Press.

Shannon, Terry, Sentinels of Our Shores, the Story of Lighthouses, Lightships, and Buoys. 1969 Golden Gate Junior Books, San Carlos, CA

Smith, Arthur, <u>Lighthouses,</u> 1971 Houghlin Mifflin, Boston, MA

"Lighthouses, Guardians of the Night," 1988 Sofidoc Production, Publisher's Choice, Video, New York, N.Y. 10001

"Lighthouses of North America," Matrix Video, Charleston, S.C. 29413-0700

Titles by Rev. Barbara Williams:

I PLEAD THE BLOOD!

IF YOU NEED HEALING... LAWYER UP!

YOU HAVE BEEN REDEEMED

YOU ARE HEALED BY AN OATH AND A PROMISE

JESUS IS THE WAY TO HEALING

7 WEEKS TO HEALTH AND HEALING (Vol. 1)

7 WEEKS TO HEALTH AND HEALING (Vol. 2)

THE MINISTRY OF THE WATCHMAN: Beacon of The Body of Christ, Keeper of The Lord's Lighthouse

GOD WANTS US TO BE PROPHETIC PEOPLE (Vol. 1)

GOD WANTS US TO BE PROPHETIC PEOPLE (Vol. 2)

7 WEEKS WITH THE GOD OF ALL COMFORT

7 WEEKS WITH JESUS

PROVERBS WISDOM FOR WOMEN PRAYER DEVOTIONAL

PROVERBS WISDOM FOR MEN PRAYER DEVOTIONAL

PRAYERS THAT AVAIL MUCH MORE: Making Known to Principalities & Powers the Manifold Wisdom of God *(Ministry of the Watchman Master Prayer Manual)*

Titles by Rev. Shirley Camp:

THE PRIZE: The High Calling and The Great Commission

HE MAKES ALL THINGS NEW: Trusting God in Seasons of Transition

AWAKE AND PUT ON STRENGTH! Being an End-time Warrior

CAN WE TALK?: About Tongues

CAN WE TALK?: About Ministering the Gift of the Holy Spirit

Order online at
ministryofthewatchman.com/store

Amazon.com/author/shirleycamp
Amazon.com/author/barbarawilliams

To receive information about
the Ministry of the Watchman, or to begin receiving
The Ministry of the Watchman's annual publication,
The Lord's Lighthouse,

Contact us: **1-800-560-9240**

The Ministry of the Watchman International
P.O. Box 43334, Cleveland, OH 44143
office@ministryofthewatchman.com

For Healing School and Miracle Service
Schedule, ministry itinerary, prophecies,
testimonies, teachings and much more, visit us
on the web at:

www.ministryofthewatchman.com

Find us on
Facebook

facebook.com/ministryofthewatchman

Nothing is Impossible with God!
JESUS WANTS TO HEAL YOU!

Join us for the Ministry of the Watchman's next

HEALING SCHOOL
& MIRACLE SERVICE

Jesus Has Healed Hundreds of People at These Miracle Meetings!

Rev. Barbara Williams has a powerful healing ministry. God has done notable miracles in her meetings such as the healing of the deaf, healing cancer, removing growths, and healing broken limbs.

God also does special miracles through the anointing released on handkerchiefs and prayer cloths. God releases miracles in the financial realm as well. Whether your need is physical, emotional or financial, Prophetess Williams will be praying for you to receive your miracle. You will want to come if you need a miracle of any kind.

FREE! ALL WELCOME!
BRING THE SICK!

For details: 1-800-560-9240

ministryofthewatchman.com

Made in United States
Orlando, FL
13 November 2023

38896432R00095